SIGNPOSTS ON THE ROAD TO EMMAUS
EXPLORING THE MASS

Julie Kavanagh is the Pastoral Resource person for the diocese of Kildare & Leighlin. She holds a Masters in Liturgical Studies from St John's University, Collegeville, Minnesota, and is a member of the Council for Liturgy (Irish Bishops' Conference). She has worked in the area of parish ministry for over twenty years, and is currently on the panel of lecturers for the National Centre for Liturgy, Maynooth, as well as being visiting lecturer at St Margaret Beaufort's Institute, Cambridge.

SIGNPOSTS ON THE ROAD TO EMMAUS

Exploring the Mass

A programme by

Julie Kavanagh

Published 2012 by
Veritas Publications
7–8 Lower Abbey Street
Dublin 1
Ireland
publications@veritas.ie
www.veritas.ie

ISBN 978 1 84730 397 4

Copyright © Julie Kavanagh, 2012

10 9 8 7 6 5 4 3 2 1

The material in this publication is protected by copyright law. Except as may be permitted by law, no part of the material may be reproduced (including by storage in a retrieval system) or transmitted in any form or by any means, adapted, rented or lent without the written permission of the copyright owners. Applications for permissions should be addressed to the publisher.

All scripture passages, unless otherwise stated, are taken from the *New Revised Standard Version Bible* © 1989, 1995 by the Division of Christian Education of National Council of the Churches of Christ in the United States of America. Used with permission. All rights reserved.
Lyrics from 'To Be Your Bread' by David Haas, text copyright © 1981, 1982 by GIA Publications Inc., 7404 S. Mason Avenue, Chicago, IL 60638. www.giamusic.com 800.442.1358. All rights reserved. Used by permission.
Lyrics from 'The Servant Song' by Richard Gillard, text copyright © 1977.

A catalogue record for this book is available from the British Library.

Designed by Dara O'Connor, Veritas
Printed in Ireland by Hudson Killeen Ltd, Dublin

Veritas books are printed on paper made from the wood pulp of managed forests. For every tree felled, at least one tree is planted, thereby renewing natural resources.

Dedication

This book is dedicated to my husband, John McHugh, and our three beautiful girls, Ellen, Kate and Róisín, with whom I have the awesome and wonderful gift of making a home of faith and love.

This wholly welcome programme seeks to energise the Catholic person in exploring their relationship with Christ and with their parish community in the celebration of the Mass. It provides an effective way of engaging with each other, as part of a local community, helping people reflect on their experience as participants in the Eucharist. The programme is short, practical and accessible. It highlights the various elements within the celebration of the Mass, and the call to action with Christ beyond the celebration, building up the Christian community and serving others with joy, particularly those in most need. It responds precisely to the encouragement by the Irish Episcopal Conference in *Share the Good News: National Directory for Catechesis in Ireland* that catechetical programmes and support material for liturgical celebrations be designed for use in the parish community (SGN 167).

Gareth Byrne, *Share the Good News: National Directory for Catechesis in Ireland*

Contents

Introduction
- About the Programme 9
- Who it is for 9
- Origin of the Programme 9
- Programme Outcomes – for Participants and for the Worshipping Community 9
- A Word of Caution 10
- *Share the Good News* 10
- Third Edition of the Roman Missal 10
- Outline of the Sessions 11
- Handouts and PowerPoint slides 11
- Overview of Individual Sessions 11
  - Overview Session One 11
  - Overview Session Two 12
  - Overview Session Three 12
  - Overview Session Four 12
- Hosting a Session 13
- This is not an 'all or nothing' programme! 14
- Reflective Session 15
- The Thing about Signposts 15

Session One
We Gather in the Footsteps of Christ 16
- Structured Overview 16
- Opening Prayer 18
- Movement 1 20
- Movement 2 20
- Movement 3 22
- Movement 4 23
- Movement 5 28
- Wrap-up & Closing Prayer 28
- Session One Handout 29

Session Two
Christ Speaks to Us in the Scriptures Today 31
- Structured Overview 31
- Opening Prayer 33
- Movement 1 35
- Movement 2 35
- Movement 3 37
- Movement 4 38
- Movement 5 41
- Wrap-up & Closing Prayer 42
- Session Two Handout 43

Session Three
Christ is Our Host 45
- Structured Overview 45
- Opening Prayer 47
- Movement 1 49
- Movement 2 49
- Movement 3 51
- Movement 4 52
- Movement 5 60
- Wrap-up & Closing Prayer 60
- Session Three Handout 61

Session Four
We are Sent to Become What We Have Received 63
- Structured Overview 63
- Opening Prayer 65
- Movement 1 67
- Movement 2 67
- Movement 3 68
- Movement 4 69
- Movement 5 76
- Wrap-Up & Closing Prayer 76
- Session Four Handout 79

A Reflective Session
- Preparation and Outline 81
- Session Material 82
- Reading I 83
- Reflection I 83
- Reading II 85
- Reflection II 86
- Reading III 88
- Reflection III 88
- Reading IV 90
- Reflection IV 90
- Closing Opportunity for Sharing 91

- Eucharistic Prayer II Handout 93

A Short Recommended Reading List 94

Acknowledgements 95

Introduction

Signposts on the Road to Emmaus: Exploring the Mass

About the Programme

Signposts on the Road to Emmaus is a four-session programme of exploration on the celebration of the Mass. Each session follows a similar pattern which accumulatively gives participants a renewed understanding of the Mass they celebrate in their own place and time. The story from St Luke's Gospel of the two disciples who encounter Jesus on the road to Emmaus forms the backdrop to each of the sessions.

The programme purposely uses an adult model of catechesis, drawing upon the lived experience of participants, sacred scripture, liturgical texts and the practical application to local celebrations of liturgy. This leads to a renewed and deepened understanding of the Mass and its celebration.

Who it is for

Signposts on the Road to Emmaus is designed to be accessible to anyone who is interested in finding out more about the Mass. Parishioners, members of parish and college liturgy groups, diocesan liturgy commissions, parish pastoral councils, parish pastoral workers, clergy and all those with responsibility for preparing liturgy will find these sessions of personal and practical benefit. Indeed, it could easily form part of a training programme for liturgy groups. This material has also been successfully used in the secondary school classroom at senior cycle level.

Origin of the Programme

Signposts on the Road to Emmaus grew out of a night of formation for liturgical ministers that took place in the Cathedral Parish in Carlow in Autumn 2005. It was subsequently taken up by a number of other parishes in the Kildare & Leighlin Diocese. From the beginning it was felt that this one-night experience could dig deeper.

The programme was expanded to four sessions as part of the Kildare & Leighlin Diocesan preparation for the International Eucharistic Congress, held in Dublin in June 2012. Over twenty presenters, working in pairs, led the programme in venues across the diocese between October 2011 and April 2012.

Programme Outcomes – for Participants and for the Worshipping Community

For participants ...
It is intended that participants will come away from the programme with a much deeper understanding and awareness of what happens at Mass and their own role in the celebration. This will, hopefully, feed into the local experience. The good practice explored in the programme can be affirmed where it is already happening and applied where it is not.

A common piece of feedback from people who have undertaken the programme is that there is a new understanding about something that they have been doing and celebrating for years. Time and time again presenters heard phrases such as, 'How come I never saw it that way before ...' or, 'I never realised that, I never thought of that ...' Both presenters and participants have spoken positively about the impact the course has had on their own participation in the Mass subsequently.

For the worshipping community ...
This is a programme that actively seeks to engage with the lived experience of participants. In the exploration of the Mass, participants are led to reflect upon how they as a worship community can and do make the movement from the ritual book of the Roman Missal to a living celebration according to that Rite.

By affirming where and how the faith community is richly celebrating the Mass and by inviting participants to consider ways in which the local celebration can be enriched, this programme has the potential to be a catalyst for deepening and strengthening the worship life of the local faith community. The programme can lead to local commitment and action to bring the learning and reflection of participants to bear on the celebration of the Mass itself.

A Word of Caution

When we gather a group of adults and then proceed to discover, learn, reflect and look to the future with them, then we had better be prepared to listen to what they have to say and to be seen to respond to it. In other words, if as part of the programme a group actively makes suggestions for enhancing the celebration of the Mass, in light of and informed by what they have shared together, then there needs to be some kind of local mechanism in place that can move these suggestions from ideas to reality. This mechanism might be a liturgy group (one that already exists or one that emerges from the course itself), a pastoral parish council, a pastoral team or another such body.

The key point is not to look for engagement with others through shared reflection, learning and suggestions and then promptly ignore them! Think ahead to how *Signposts on the Road to Emmaus* might be facilitated to positively feed into the worship community beyond the programme itself.

Share the Good News

This programme comes in the footsteps of the Irish Episcopal Conference's National Directory for Catechesis in Ireland, *Share the Good News* (Veritas, 2010). This document presents a vision of catechesis that spans the whole arc of one's life. It provides a framework and principles for the presentation of the Good News of Jesus Christ in the circumstances of people's life and culture. In doing so it extends an invitation to develop resources to this end. I very much hope that this programme finds a place among a wide range of emerging resources in response to this invitation.

Third Edition of the Roman Missal

This programme takes into account the texts of the Mass according to the third edition of the Roman Missal. The material includes an explanation of some of the changes to the Mass, particularly in relation to the responses of the people.

OUTLINE OF THE SESSIONS

Each session is designed to last for approximately 75–90 minutes. Given the methodology employed by the programme, an optimum number of participants is between fifteen and thirty-five people, though it has been used with greater and fewer than these numbers.

It begins with a welcome and opening prayer. It then proceeds in five movements before concluding with a final prayer. The movements are as follows:

> *Movement 1 – Paying attention to our own human experience*
> *Movement 2 – Hearing and reflecting on a particular phase of the Emmaus story*
> *Movement 3 – Applying that story to our own experience as a praying community*
> *Movement 4 – Exploring a particular phase of the Sunday Mass*
> *Movement 5 – Making concrete suggestions for our local practice*

HANDOUTS AND POWERPOINT SLIDES

Each session comes with its own handouts. These are designed in such a way as to offer presenters some flexibility in the material. In some instances a presenter may refer to material on the handout as 'take home reading' or points for consideration in the future, by a liturgy group or other body, rather than devote time to it within the session itself.

The handouts are reproduced in this book at the end of each session and can be photocopied for local use. Alternatively the handouts can be found on the following link: veritasbooksonline.com/signpostsontheroadtoemmaus/resources

A set of PowerPoint slides is available for each session for those who would like to avail of this further aid. Again these can be accessed and downloaded on the link above. Similarly, Eucharistic Prayer II, which appears on p. 93 of this book, can also be found at this link.

OVERVIEW OF INDIVIDUAL SESSIONS

SESSION ONE – WE GATHER IN THE FOOTSTEPS OF CHRIST

This session explores the Introductory Rites of the Mass. Following the welcome and opening prayer, the session invites participants to reflect on the human experience of gathering, noting why people gather and why some gatherings are more significant than others. The material then moves to the story of Emmaus and the encounter of the two disciples on the road with Jesus. Reflecting on this experience, the group begins to make connections with this encounter and our own story on a Sunday morning as we begin to gather as a praying community. Participants are invited to reflect upon what helps them to feel welcome and part of the celebration while moving to view the gathered congregation as 'the Body of Christ'.

The Introductory Rites are then explored in detail, looking at their function, texts and enactment while highlighting specific good practices. The final movement invites people to reflect on their own local experience, affirming good practice and making suggestions for future growth. Participants are sent out from the session in a spirit of prayer.

Session Two – Christ Speaks to Us in the Scriptures Today

The second session explores the Liturgy of the Word. Again after a welcome and opening prayer, participants begin by exploring the human experience of listening and story sharing which is vital to our understanding of this phase of the Mass. We hear from and reflect on the next part of the Emmaus story, again applying that reflection to our own experience of receiving and listening to God's word as a community. Emphasis is given to how, when the scriptures are read in church, God is speaking to God's people today.

The Liturgy of the Word is then explored with particular reference to its structure and enactment. The opportunity is also taken to highlight changes in text in accordance with the revised Missal, for example, 'The Word of the Lord' and some changes within the Nicene Creed. Again suggestions for good practice during the Liturgy of the Word are given. These include the use of pace, music, the Lectionary book, silence, the Gospel procession and a consideration of the Prayer of the Faithful. Time is given for people to reflect on their own local practice and again to affirm what is happening while making suggestions for future practice. Prayer once more concludes the session.

Session Three – Christ is Our Host

In this third session, participants move deeper into the Emmaus story and the celebration of the Mass. Our focus in this session is the first two parts of the Liturgy of the Eucharist, from the Preparation of the Gifts to the Great Amen. (The Communion Rite is explored in the next session.) Participants enter into the session welcomed and nourished by a shared prayer. Time is then given to pay attention to the experience of sharing significant meals, highlighting the hallmarks of such meals and the preparation undertaken for these meals by both host and guests.

The Emmaus story deepens our understanding, noting the movement of Christ from being the guest to being the host of the meal shared. Attention is given to the importance of human hungers, of bread itself as the staff of life and to the moment of recognition and continued remembrance on the part of the two disciples.

These themes are then translated in broad terms to the Sunday experience before moving to a more detailed exploration of the Liturgy of the Eucharist, naming the Eucharistic actions of taking, blessing, breaking and sharing, and focusing on the first two of these actions in the Preparation of the Gifts and the Eucharistic Prayer. Here we again find referencing and explanations for some changes to text as found in the new edition of the Missal. Local practice is, in turn, reflected upon for future enhancement of the celebration.

Session Four – We are Sent to Become What We Have Received

The final session draws the account from Emmaus to a close and explores the final stages of the Mass, namely the Communion Rite and the Concluding Rites. As in all the sessions, the first movement is one of welcome and prayer. Participants are then invited to focus and reflect on the notion of personally responding to a call to action in their own lives. This reflection leads to recognising and naming the response of the disciples at Emmaus to their encounter with Christ – how it led them back to Jerusalem as witnesses to Christ, prepared to actively share in the mission of Christ. Again this calls us to make the link with our own Sunday experience and how we are continually being sent from the Mass to live what we have celebrated.

The session then proceeds by unpacking the journey of the Communion Rite, with its rich scriptural allusions and the gift of Christ of himself to the Church in the Eucharist, which is at the centre of this rite.

Finally, the Concluding Rites and their journey are explored with an invitational focus on the call to go and be what we have received. There is perhaps no other way to end a programme of reflection on the Mass than in a prayerful missioning of participants to live Eucharist.

Hosting a Session

Leaders

The programme is designed to walk leaders easily through each session, giving them the structure, process and material to navigate their way. The person or people who lead the sessions do not need, therefore, to be experts in liturgy. They do however need to a) have the appropriate skills to work with adults; and b) have the willingness and capacity to present the material. This material is faith-based. It goes without saying, then, that any leader or leaders need to be people of faith.

Two people typically worked together in each venue when this programme was piloted in the Kildare & Leighlin Diocese. This approach offered leaders the support of a co-worker in the preparation, delivery and review of the programme. In turn it offered participants the variety of another voice and presence. The programme, however, is not dependent on having two leaders.

Hospitality

Some time and thought should always be given to how a session will be hosted from beginning to end. One of the hallmarks of the programme, from preparation, delivery and beyond, should be hospitality. From the set-up of the room itself and the readiness of leaders for any given session, to the welcome of the people as they come into the room, a sense of hospitality and a sense that something of value and importance is about to take place in this space should be communicated.

Once a session begins, a spirit of hospitality should continue. This can be demonstrated by how people are treated and engaged with throughout the session. People should have a real and tangible sense of being welcomed, respected and listened to throughout their experience of the programme.

The hospitality can flow beyond the session through the provision of a cup of tea at the end. This gives people an opportunity to continue their conversations with one another in a relaxed setting while facilitating those who need to leave to do so.

Set-up
Try to ensure that the room in which the programme is taking place is appropriate for the participants. It should be comfortable, warm and conducive to the exploration that is about to take place. Make sure the room is as you want it before you begin. Try to avoid setting it up as a classroom. Seating set out in a semi-circle seems to work best for engaging people in conversation.

It can be helpful to have a focus for participants during the opening prayer. This might be as simple as a table upon which is placed a cloth, candle, cross/icon, a bible or other appropriate objects. Again try to have this in place before people arrive. This will help to create an air of expectancy and readiness among those who have come.

Likewise try to have any technology that you are using ready for action. This is especially important if you are using PowerPoint slides. It helps whoever is leading the session greatly if they are not stressing about whether a computer will behave or not! It can also be very welcoming and reassuring to participants to come into a room that is already displaying a welcome slide for the session.

Beginning the session
Some simple steps can be taken at the beginning of each session to help participants move into the material in a relaxed and open manner.
1. Welcome people at the beginning and establish a friendly atmosphere among the group.
2. Introduce yourself.
3. Place the session in the context of the full programme reminding people as appropriate what has been explored to date.
4. Say what will be explored in the particular session.
5. Give people an opportunity to say hello to one another.
6. Let people know the finish time and whether or not a cup of tea/coffee is being offered at the end.

Prayer
The prayer experiences in a session are important elements that require preparation. The opening prayer sets the tone for what is to follow, reminding us that all we do, we do in the name of the Lord. It serves to unite participants in a spirit of shared attentiveness to God and God's ongoing presence in the midst of all our endeavours and explorations. The closing prayer grounds us once more in this truth. Participants can be invited to lead some elements of the prayer before the prayer begins. To this end, those leading the session should reflect on these prayer texts ahead of time and how they are going to be prayed in the particular context. The use of silence within the prayer also needs consideration.

THIS IS NOT AN 'ALL OR NOTHING' PROGRAMME!
Obviously the best way of getting the most out of the programme is to come with an open heart and mind to each of the four sessions. However, if a participant is unable to come to an individual session, they should in no way feel that this prohibits them from coming to the

other sessions. Each session can stand independently. It is helpful to communicate this when promoting the programme.

Reflective Session

The final chapter of this book goes back to the very beginning of this programme and the originating 'Evening of Reflection for Liturgical Ministers' that first took place in Carlow Cathedral Parish. This session focuses on the story of Emmaus. Journeying through it in a reflective manner, the session seeks to help participants make tangible links between that Gospel narrative and our contemporary celebration and local experience of the Mass. It is not intended as a catechesis on the structure and ritual action of the Mass, rather it is a prayerful way of giving liturgical ministers and others an opportunity to look to the Mass through a particular lens. This session is offered here as a further resource to people.

The Thing about Signposts

Signposts are meant to point us in a particular direction, to lead us down a particular path, while in some way naming what we hope to find at our destination. My hope in writing this programme is that it will indeed offer signposts for those who participate in it. I hope that in journeying with the two disciples on that road out of Jerusalem to Emmaus, and back to Jerusalem, people will discover the many insights into the Mass that that road trip offers us. In exploring and teasing out each signpost along the way, may we enter deeper into what is at the heart of what we are about as a Christian community: the Eucharist – its enduring gift, its celebration and the life to which it calls each and every one of us.

The two disciples ended their journey where they started. Whenever we set out to explore the Mass, we eventually come back to the starting point – our active participation in the Mass itself. For those who engage in this programme I hope that it can offer a glimpse of what T. S. Elliot imagined …

> We shall not cease from exploration
> And the end of all our exploring
> Will be to arrive where we started
> And know the place for the first time.
> (*from* 'Four Quartets')

SESSION ONE

We Gather in the Footsteps of Christ

STRUCTURED OVERVIEW

PURPOSE OF THE SESSION

To explore the celebration and enactment of the Introductory Rites of the Mass in the local setting, bringing insights from the human experience of gathering, the scriptural encounter on the road to Emmaus and the Introductory Rites themselves as given in the Roman Missal. This will lead to practical suggestions for local enhancement of the celebration of these Rites.

*SESSION OUTLINE**

Welcome & Introductions
Opening Prayer . . . . (10 min)

Movement 1:
Paying attention to our own experience of gathering . . . . (5 min)

Movement 2:
Hearing the story and reflecting on the gathering at Emmaus . . . . (10 min)

Movement 3:
Applying the story to our own experience as a praying community . . . . . . (10 min)

Movement 4:
Exploring the liturgical action of gathering on a Sunday . . . . (30 min)

Movement 5:
Making concrete suggestions for our own local experience . . . . (10 min)

Closing Prayer
Cuppa

(1 hr 15 min)

* The movements move quickly into one another with the bulk of the material being found in Movement 4. The time indicators are guides and are designed to be flexible. Organisers and participants might agree to give 1 hr 30 min to the session, which obviously would give extra time to some elements, particularly Movement 4. Some groups may wish to remain in conversation for even longer.

CHECKLIST IMMEDIATELY PRIOR TO A SESSION

- ☐ Set up the room in a warm and inviting manner, with chairs in a semi-circle rather than lecture style.
- ☐ Prepare a prayer focus in the room, for example a covered table with a candle, icon/cross, Bible.
- ☐ Have any technology needed ready for use before people arrive.
- ☐ Have any handouts/flip chart stand, paper and pens ready for use.
- ☐ Delegate any readings or other tasks to be done before the session begins.
- ☐ Welcome people as they arrive.

Session One: We Gather in the Footsteps of Christ

When the session begins
- ☐ Welcome people formally to the session.
- ☐ Introduce yourself and your role in the session.
- ☐ Introduce the session in the context of the programme 'Signposts on the Road to Emmaus' and the purpose of this first session.
- ☐ Let people know the end time and whether or not a cup of tea/coffee is being offered at the end.
- ☐ Give people an opportunity to greet one another.
- ☐ Introduce the Opening Prayer – this can include the lighting of a candle.

enten.

Initiative led by Bishop Denis & programme compiled by Julie Kavanagh of F.D.S.

Philip → Pastoral Worker
Ruairi → Administrator
4 part series which consists of an exploration -
Exploration of the Mass

Tea & Coffee at end.

Opening prayer. → Richard.

Signposts on the Road to Emmaus

Opening Prayer

Invitation to Prayer

We gather this day as followers of Christ, following in the footsteps of one who has called us, who has loved us and who has promised to be with us in every footstep of our journey. He told us, 'Where two or three are gathered in my name, I am there'. And so we welcome Christ into our very midst and in gratitude we mark ourselves with the sign of faith to which he has called each one of us: In the name of the Father and of the Son and of the Holy Spirit. Amen.

Focus

We welcome these words of scripture into our hearts and into our prayer to God.

> Before I formed you in the womb I knew you, and before you were born I consecrated you.
>
> (JEREMIAH 1:5)*

> For it was you who formed my inward parts; you knit me together in my mother's womb. I praise you, for I am fearfully and wonderfully made.
>
> (PSALM 139:13-14)

> Whoever walks in integrity walks securely.
>
> (PROVERBS 10:9)

Pause

Scripture — Mary

> After John had been arrested, Jesus went into Galilee. There he proclaimed the gospel from God saying, 'The time is fulfilled, and the kingdom of God is close at hand. Repent, and believe the Gospel.'
> As he was walking along by the Lake of Galilee he saw Simon and Simon's brother Andrew casting a net in the lake – for they were fishermen. And Jesus said to them, 'Come after me and I will make you into fishers of people.' And at once they left their nets and followed him.
>
> (MARK 1:14-18, NEW JERUSALEM BIBLE)

---

* All scripture passages are taken from the *New Revised Standard Version Bible*, unless otherwise stated.

This page may be photocopied

*Reflection** Betty.

Life unfolds
a petal at a time
slowly.

The beauty of the process is crippled
when I try to hurry growth.
Life has its inner rhythm
which must be respected.
It cannot be rushed or hurried.

Like daylight stepping out of darkness,
like morning creeping out of night
life unfolds slowly
a petal at a time
like a flower opening to the sun,
slowly.

God's call unfolds
a Word at a time
slowly.

A disciple is not made in a hurry.
Slowly I become like the One
to whom I am listening.

Life unfolds
a petal at a time
like you and I
becoming followers of Jesus,
disciple into a new way of living
deeply and *slowly.*

Be patient with life's unfolding petals.
If you hurry the bud it withers.
If you hurry life it limps.
Each unfolding is a teaching
a movement of grace
filled with silent pauses
breathtaking beauty
tears and heartaches.

Life unfolds
a petal at a time
deeply and *slowly.*

May it come to pass!

Quiet Moment

Prayer
Creator God,
You who formed us in our mother's womb
and who sent your Son with the message of the Good News of your kingdom,
    grant us
the patience to listen for your call to us,
the wisdom to understand the life to which it leads us,
and the love to embrace the journey with joyful and generous hearts.

We ask this in the name of the one in whose footsteps we follow, your Son, our Lord Jesus Christ. Amen.

---

* Taken from *The Song of the Seed: A Monastic Way of Tending the Soul*, by Macrina Wiederkeher (New York: HarperCollins, 1995), p. 120.

This page may be photocopied

SIGNPOSTS ON THE ROAD TO EMMAUS

Movement 1 (5 min)
Paying attention to our own experience of gathering

The material begins by focusing the theme of 'gathering' around a 'human' experience of gathering. The leader of the session invites participants to name a few examples of such gatherings. The following questions can be drawn upon for this part.

> **Leader suggestion:** If possible, record the answers on a flip chart.

GROUP CONVERSATION

» *Where and when do we see people gathering?*
  The leader might brainstorm instances. Examples might include at pop concerts, meetings, family reunions and meals, the pub, a ticket office, dole queues, bus stops, airports, shopping centres, funeral homes, sports venues, hospitals ... Once the participants have exhausted the examples, choose a few of the given examples. Work through them in greater detail using 'who, what, where, when, why, what if ...' questions.

» *What makes gatherings significant for the people who gather? What are the key ingredients?*
  Answers might include personal involvement/impact, caring about the people with whom we gather, having a common purpose/need ...

Drawing the feedback together
Having processed the questions with the group, the leader reminds participants what they have collectively expressed as key understandings of human gatherings.

Movement 2 (10 min) PP
Hearing the story and reflecting on the gathering at Emmaus

> **Leader suggestion:** Before the session begins, have someone ready to read this Gospel passage, using a Bible.

We have begun to explore our experience of Gathering. Let us turn our attention to a biblical example of a gathering: We hear now from a passage from St Luke's Gospel.

READING   John

> A reading from the Holy Gospel according to Luke (24:13-18)
>
> Now on that same day two of them were going to a village called Emmaus, about seven miles from Jerusalem, and talking with each other about all these things that had happened. While they were talking and discussing, Jesus himself came near and went with them, but their eyes were kept from recognising him.

SESSION ONE: WE GATHER IN THE FOOTSTEPS OF CHRIST

> And he said to them, 'What are you discussing with each other while you walk along?' They stood still, looking sad. Then one of them, whose name was Cleopas, answered him, 'Are you the only stranger in Jerusalem who does not know the things that have taken place there in these days?'
> He asked them, 'What things?' They replied, 'The things about Jesus of Nazareth ...'
>
> The Gospel of the Lord.

Reflection

This reflection can be done conversationally/interactively with the group. Leaders are invited to make the material their own.

This is the beginning of a story with which we are very familiar – the Emmaus story. But perhaps for the next while we might sit with this opening part of the story and tease out what it can speak to us of 'gathering'.

'Now on that same day two of them were going to a village ...' We enter into the story of these two – in the middle of a journey, from Jerusalem to a place about seven miles away, Emmaus.

Who were these two on the road? We are not really told much about them. We are given the name Cleopas, the one and only time he is mentioned in the Gospel accounts. But we are not told anything about his companion: was it a man or a woman; perhaps they were a married couple; perhaps they were two men. We just don't know.

What are they doing? They are talking about what had been happening and the events in Jerusalem. They are full of the news of the day.

How are they feeling as they discuss the news of the day? Remember, these two had gone in hope to Jerusalem. They were now returning to Emmaus filled with disappointment and sadness, no doubt confused and with heavy hearts.

Today, in our meetings with others, what might the news be? What are we hearing in the news these days: perhaps of natural disasters, bailouts, job losses, drugs, political upheaval and fallouts, world, national and local events of importance and interest to us.

> **Leader suggestion:** Headlines from the week's papers might be read out to participants.

We talk about the events of our days and in doing so we are really trying to figure out how this impacts us, who we are in all of this – individually and collectively.

We return to our story of the two on the road. A stranger comes along the road and breaks into their journey. This stranger engages with them, he wants to become part of their conversation, he risks taking the initiative to enter into relationship with them.

He asks them a question: 'What are you discussing …?' They could reject him, turn away from him, or tell him firmly to mind his own business. But they don't. They allow him in. They welcome him into their midst. We, with the benefit of hindsight, know what gift they give to themselves as a result of their action of hospitality, and this hospitality is the hallmark of Christian gathering. It is the first action, the first impulse, the first movement of every Christian gathering; the movement outward towards another, a movement of welcome, inclusion, reverence. This is a key understanding to carry with us as we come together to worship our God.

Movement 3 (10 min)
Applying the story to our own experience as a praying community

Again this can be done conversationally with the group.

Refection
Now let's stop and let's imagine our Sunday experience. As we make our way to church on a Sunday or Saturday evening, we are all coming from different places with some common experiences and some unique ones. We make the journey to our churches from all different starting points, carrying different life experiences and emotions. Our minds can be full of the happenings and encounters of the week – global, local and personal – but we move in a common direction.

And at some point in our journey towards Mass we begin to meet one another – getting out of the car, moving through the door of the church, as we bless ourselves with holy water, as we take our seat in the pew. We find ourselves alongside others, young and old, friend, neighbour, acquaintance and stranger. How is that meeting? How do we see that stranger? Do we acknowledge them? Is it part of our consciousness even to say hello, to greet them?

In the story, the two did not know it was Christ. We are told that their eyes were kept from recognising Jesus; something within them prevented them from recognising the risen Lord. Yet they welcomed him into their story. They welcomed this stranger in their midst. This is a key point in Luke's story: welcoming the stranger is a key to celebrating Eucharist. Just think of the lost opportunity if they had turned their backs. Think of what they would have missed out on if they had told him to keep to himself.

These two, whoever they are, have given us a model of communion and ministry. In being welcoming, in including the stranger in our journey we are welcoming Christ.

On a Sunday we get to welcome Christ *in the congregation,* in the assembly. We are the Body of Christ.

> 'For where two or three are gathered in my name, I am there among them.' (Matthew 18:20)

SESSION ONE: WE GATHER IN THE FOOTSTEPS OF CHRIST

When we gather to pray, Christ is present. In the midst of that assembly we get to meet the risen Lord week in and week out. From the first moments of the liturgy Christ is present. From these first moments we are called into communion with Christ and with one another.

Our invitation on a Sunday when we gather to celebrate Mass is to reach out and welcome Christ in our midst. This impacts what we do even before Mass begins and what we do during the Introductory Rites of the Mass.

Reflection Questions for the Group PP
» What helps me to feel welcome to and part of the Mass?
» What difference does it/can it make to see the congregation, as a whole, as the Body of Christ?

Leader suggestion: If time allows, have people share with a neighbour and then hear back from the group.

Movement 4 (Part 1 – 10 min; Part 2 – 20 min)
Exploring the liturgical action of gathering on a Sunday PP

This material is given in two parts – Part 1 and Part 2. The first part looks at what happens before the Mass even begins. The second part addresses specifically the Introductory Rites.

PART 1
PREPARING TO PRAY AS A COMMUNITY

When we gather to celebrate the Mass there is an amount of groundwork that needs to be done collectively and individually.
Even before Mass begins, as a local faith community we are invited to create:
- A welcoming environment
- A welcoming presence
- A sense of expectancy and preparation – that something of deep importance is about to be celebrated
- A sense of community
- A space for people to gather as a community and worship their God together.

» How might we do this in our own places?
» What does/would help do this?

Leader suggestion: The leader asks for people's responses to the questions above. He/she may tease it out further by drawing on some of the following, offering suggestions for practice. Alternatively the leader might refer people to the handout as something to read and act upon beyond the session. Responses might be recorded on a flip chart.

Some suggestions for exploration
- Is the liturgical space clean, uncluttered, inviting, accessible? (For example, for people who use wheelchairs, for people who are hearing impaired.)

- Are passers-by given any sense of invitation to come in and worship from any notice on the outside of the church building?
- Is there a well-informed and well-presented notice board?
- Do the 'things' of the liturgy – the vestments, ritual books, vessels and symbols – communicate the dignity and importance of our celebration?
- Are people welcomed as they come into the church?
- Do people have what they need to celebrate the liturgy, i.e. music sheets, candles at the Easter vigil …?
- Are they given any necessary preparation before Mass begins, i.e. new music, specific instructions?
- Does the parish ever give people an opportunity to greet one another before the beginning of Mass?
- Does a member of the community ever introduce the Mass?
- Does the liturgical space communicate the stage of the liturgical year currently being celebrated in the life of the Church?
- Have enough ministers been assigned for a rich celebration, have they been given all necessary instruction and formation, and are they ready to carry out their ministry in a spirit of hospitality?

Part 2
Introductory Rites

We turn our attention to the actual Introductory Rites. The Introductory Rites include everything that happens from the moment we stand together with the rest of the worshipping community at Mass until we sit down for the first time.

The function of the rites is to enable the community, coming together from a multiplicity of concerns and a variety of ways of life, to become aware of itself again as a gathered community, alert and ready to listen to the word and to celebrate the sacrament.
(*Celebrating the Mystery of Faith*, National Centre for Liturgy, 2011)

The above is what we want to achieve in the Introductory Rites through the journey of these rites.

> ***Leader suggestion:*** The following can be either presented straight or mapped out via a brainstorm with participants, in response to a question such as 'What are the different parts that we find in the Introductory Rites of the Mass?'

This journey is as follows:
- Entrance Procession and Chant ♪
- Greeting
- Penitential Act *or* blessing and sprinkling of water
- Kyrie (omitted if 'Lord have mercy' already used or if sprinkling used) ♪
- Gloria ♪
- Collect (opening prayer).

Session One: We Gather in the Footsteps of Christ

Leader Background Material and Notes

The amount of the following material covered will depend on time. Again it is intended that leaders explore the parts of the Introductory Rites in a conversational style with participants, making the notes their own. The key parts to highlight in the following are the entrance procession and chant with, at times, use of incense, a mention of posture, and the structure of the opening prayer. Other items can be covered depending on time, or participants can be referred to the handout for further information.

For ease of presentation, suggestions are interspersed with the material in this session.

Entrance Procession

The entrance procession through the body of people is a visible and strong reminder to us that we gather as the Body of Christ. The procession through the assembly reminds us that Christ gathers us into one and that it is this community who celebrates the Mass, in communion with Christ and with one another. Priest, ministers and people begin in a moment of convergence and unity.

Some suggestions
- Try to have a procession through the people regularly at Sunday Mass. If processing, the order is as follows: server with thurible (if using incense); servers with candles, and between them the cross-bearer; other servers; a reader (or deacon) who may carry the Book of the Gospels; the priest celebrant.
- Occasionally other symbols may be processed in. These might highlight an aspect of the readings or the occasion/feast/time of the liturgical year. (If done, the processing of symbols takes place at this point of the Mass rather than during the Preparation of the Gifts.)
- If carrying incense, after the priest has venerated the altar with a kiss, the altar and people are incensed. The use of incense helps greatly to engage the senses in our worship.

Entrance Chant ♪

The opening chant or hymn unites us in one voice from the opening moments of our liturgy. It helps to gather us into a community. This hymn replaces a one-sentence antiphon that appears in the Missal for the Mass of the day.

Some suggestions
- Encourage the choir to use music in the entrance procession that the assembly can sing and which sets the tone of the season or feast that they are celebrating
- The sung text can echo the readings, feast or antiphon of the day, or speak to the action of gathering.

A Mention of Posture during the Introductory Rites

When we gather on a Sunday, we get to greet the Risen Lord in our midst – Christ, present in the assembly, in the priest-celebrant, in the Word and in the Eucharist. This is a joyful event. It proclaims that we are a resurrection people. The posture for greeting another is one of standing. The appropriate posture, therefore, for the duration of the Introductory Rites is that of standing. We articulate both our welcome of Christ and our joy in the resurrection through the medium of our bodies as we stand.

Greeting

After making the Sign of the Cross together, the priest and people exchange a formal greeting, both acknowledging and evoking the presence of Christ in their midst. The style of the greeting is both warm and reverent.

The response to 'The Lord be with you' is the first change that people have encountered with the introduction of the third edition of the Roman Missal.
(Leaders might simply refer people to the handout for subsequent reading rather than going through the following, depending on time and circumstance.)

> 'And with your spirit' is the literal translation of what we find in the Latin text *et cum spiritu tuo*. This translation is already found in others languages, for example German, Italian, French and Spanish.
>
> The source for this dialogue between priest and people is very much Scripture. In four letters of St Paul he uses the following greetings: Galatians 6:18 – May the grace of our Lord Jesus Christ be with your spirit; Philippians 4:23 – The grace of the Lord Jesus Christ be with your spirit; 2 Timothy 4:22 – The Lord be with your spirit; Philemon 13:25 – Grace be with all of you. Similar greetings can be found in the Old Testament.
>
> What does 'your spirit' mean? It is not a reference to the Holy Spirit, though it is spoken by people who live according to that Spirit. For St Paul, the spirit is our spiritual part that is closest to God. '*And with your spirit*' is about having the spirit or mind of Christ as your guiding light, as what guides us through the day – a Christian spirit. It reminds us that when we gather for Mass, it is our whole selves that pray, not just our minds.
>
> While it will sound unfamiliar to us, this greeting and response captures our biblical roots. It recognises the spirit that is among us as Christians, a spirit that we must live, and, in greeting one another, it proclaims the presence of Christ among us.
>
> This greeting occurs elsewhere in the Mass and each time is accompanied by the response '*And with your spirit*'.

The greeting can, if appropriate, be followed by a brief and well-prepared introduction that can help set the tone for the entire celebration.

Penitential Act

The penitential act during Mass acknowledges that we are sinners, while rejoicing in God's never-ending mercy and love. There are three options. The third form is a litany of praise, addressed to Christ our redeemer. These invocations, or those modelled on them, focus on Christ and his mercy (rather than on our sinfulness). People will notice some change to the text of the first form, the Confiteor, with the introduction of the new edition of the Roman Missal. Again it is translating directly the Latin text.

I confess to almighty God and to you, my brothers and sisters,
that I have greatly sinned *— The words of David to God in 1 Chronicles 21:8*
in my thoughts and in my words,
in what I have done and in what I have failed to do,
And, striking their breast, they say:
through my fault, through my fault, through my most grievous fault; *— Already retained in the Irish language; an example of the Roman use of triplets*

Then they continue:
therefore I ask blessed Mary ever-Virgin,
all the Angels and Saints,
and you, my brothers and sisters, to pray for me to the Lord our God.

Rite of Blessing and Sprinkling of Water

The penitential act may be replaced by the occasional use of a rite of blessing and sprinkling of water. This action reminds us of our common baptism and is therefore especially appropriate during the Easter Season or when there is reference to baptism in the readings or on a particular feast day, for example the Feast of the Baptism of Our Lord. Again it is a visible reminder of our common identity as the baptised. This shared baptism gathers us together.

Some suggestions
- If this rite is to be used, let it be a lavish action, taking in the full assembly by way of its route, being generous in its sharing and, if possible, using music that speaks of water/baptism to accompany it.

Gloria ♪

The Gloria is prescribed on Sundays outside of Advent and Lent as well as on Solemnities and feasts that appear on the Calendar. The Gloria is a joyful hymn of praise of God – an appropriate way to begin our celebration in which we offer praise and thanks to God. There are a number of changes to this text in the new Missal, following very closely the Latin original. Within it we see an expansion of our address to God.

Glory to God in the highest,
and **on earth peace to people of good will.**   *Echoing the song of the angels over Bethlehem*
We praise you,   *The five actions of the Mass – praise, bless, adore, glorify, thank*
we bless you,   *These actions were condensed in the previous version*
we adore you,
we glorify you,
we give you thanks for your great glory,
Lord God, heavenly King,
O God, almighty Father.

Lord Jesus Christ, Only Begotten Son,   *Five titles of Christ*
Lord God, Lamb of God, Son of the Father,
you take away the sins of the world, have mercy on us;
you take away the sins of the world, receive our prayer;   *Creates a triplet – part of Roman style*
you are seated at the right hand of the Father, have mercy on us.
For you alone are the Holy One, you alone are the Lord,
you alone are the Most High,
Jesus Christ, with the Holy Spirit, in the glory of God the Father.

Some suggestions
- Try to have a parish-sung setting of the Gloria that conveys its sense of joy and which can be sung by the assembly, at least in its refrain.

The Collect or Opening Prayer

The goal of the Collect is to gather our prayers into one. Like all our prayers in the liturgy, this prayer is addressed to God the Father, through Christ and in the Holy Spirit. It has a four-fold pattern: invitation, silence, prayer and assent (Amen). While there is a pause for silence within the Penitential Act, the silence within the Collect is the first opportunity in the liturgy for a longer period of silence and is a valuable moment for creating a sense of unity within the silence.

Some suggestions
- Ask your priest celebrant to allow the rhythm of this prayer to speak
- Look at other places for silence in the liturgy and see if you can develop the gift that silence offers in the liturgy.

Movement 5 (10 min or to the end)
Making concrete suggestions for our own local experience

> ***Leader suggestion:*** Make sure to record what people say and to bring the responses to an appropriate forum for action.

» In light of what we have explored tonight, are there one or two things you would like to affirm in what we are doing as a worshipping community/parish?
» Are there one or two things you might suggest that we should try to do in our worshipping community/parish?
» If time allows, have participants chat about the above for a few minutes with a neighbour and then hear from the wider group. Otherwise process the questions with the group immediately.
» Let people know that you will pass on what has been recommended to the local parish for the awareness of those who prepare this liturgy.

WRAP-UP & CLOSING PRAYER

LEADER NOTE: CHECKLIST FOR CLOSE OF SESSION
- ☐ Remind people of what they have explored in the session
- ☐ Thank people for giving of their time and themselves in the session
- ☐ Let participants know when the next session of 'Signposts on the Road to Emmaus' will be taking place
- ☐ Announce what the focus of the next session will be: the celebration of the Liturgy of the Word
- ☐ Invite people to stay for a cup of tea/coffee where applicable
- ☐ Lead or invite another to bring the session to a close with a final prayer.

CLOSING PRAYER
Loving God,
You guard our coming and our going.
As we gathered in your name,
may we depart from here
bearing your presence to all we encounter
as we seek to live in faith, hope and love.

Glory be to the Father, and to the Son, and to the Holy Spirit, as it was in the beginning, is now and ever shall be, world without end. Amen.

Session One Handout

WE GATHER IN THE FOOTSTEPS OF CHRIST

> 'For where two or three are gathered in my name; I am there among them.'
> (Matthew 18:20)

Preparing to Pray as a Community

As a local faith community we are invited to create:

- A welcoming environment
- A welcoming presence
- A sense of expectancy and preparation – that something of deep importance is about to be celebrated
- A sense of community
- A space for people to gather as a community to worship their God.

Questions to consider before we begin to celebrate together

- Is the liturgical space clean, uncluttered, inviting and accessible?
- Are passers-by given any sense of invitation to come in and worship from any notice on the outside of the church building?
- Is there a well-informed and well-presented notice board?
- Do the 'items' of the liturgy – the vestments, ritual books, vessels and symbols – communicate the dignity and importance of our celebration?
- Are people welcomed as they come into the church?
- Do people have what they need to celebrate the liturgy, i.e. music sheets, candles at the Easter vigil …?
- Does the parish ever give people an opportunity to greet one another before the beginning of Mass?
- Does a member of the community ever introduce the Mass?
- Does the liturgical space communicate the stage of the liturgical year currently being celebrated in the life of the Church?
- Have enough ministers been assigned for a rich celebration of the Mass?

This page may be photocopied

Lord Jesus Christ, Only Begotten Son,
Lord God, Lamb of God, Son of the Father

Five titles of Christ

you take away the sins of the world, have mercy on us;
you take away the sins of the world, receive our prayer;
you are seated at the right hand of the Father, have mercy on us.

Creates a triplet – Roman style

For you alone are the Holy One, you alone are the Lord,
you alone are the Most High,
Jesus Christ, with the Holy Spirit, in the glory of God the Father.

The Collect or Opening prayer

The goal of the Collect is to gather our prayers into one. Like all our prayers in the liturgy, this prayer is addressed to God the Father, through Christ and in the Holy Spirit. It has a four-fold pattern: invitation, silence, prayer and assent (Amen). This is an important opportunity for silence in the liturgy and is a valuable moment for creating a sense of unity within the silence.

In the year ahead why not …

- Consider the posture of the assembly during the Introductory Rites
- Use an opening procession and on occasion incense the altar and people
- Explore using a sung Kyrie, at least, during Advent and Lent
- Use a sprinkling rite during Easter and at other appropriate times
- Allow for silence within the Opening Prayer/Collect.

Further Reading

National Centre for Liturgy, *Celebrating the Mystery of Faith* (Dublin: Veritas, 2011)

National Centre for Liturgy, *The New Missal: Explaining the Changes* (Dublin: Veritas, 2011)

International Eucharistic Congress 2012, *The Eucharist: Communion With Christ and With One Another: Theological and Pastoral Reflections in Preparation for the 50th International Eucharistic Congress* (Dublin: Veritas, 2011)

What does 'your spirit' mean? It is not a reference to the Holy Spirit, though it is spoken by people who live according to that Spirit. For St Paul, the spirit is our spiritual part that is closest to God. **'And with your spirit'** is about having the spirit or mind of Christ as your guiding light, as what guides us through the day – a Christian spirit. It reminds us that when we gather for Mass, it is our whole selves that pray, not just our minds.

While it will sound unfamiliar to us, this greeting and response captures our biblical roots. It recognises the spirit that is among us as Christians, a spirit that we must live and, in greeting one another, it proclaims the presence of Christ among us.

This greeting occurs four times in the Mass and each time is accompanied by the response *'And with your spirit'*.

I confess to almighty God and to you, my brothers and sisters,
that I have greatly sinned
in my thoughts and in my words,
in what I have done and in what I have failed to do,
And, striking their breast, they say:
**through my fault, through my fault,
through my most grievous fault;**
Then they continue:
therefore I ask blessed Mary ever-Virgin,
all the Angels and Saints,
and you, my brothers and sisters, to pray for me to the Lord our God.

The words of David to God in 1 Chronicles 21:8

Already retained in the Irish language; an example of the Roman use of triplets

Glory to God in the highest,
and **on earth peace to people of good will.**
**We praise you,
we bless you,
we adore you,
we glorify you,
we give you thanks for your great glory,**

Echoing the song of the angels over Bethlehem

The five actions of the Mass – praise, bless, adore, glorify, thank
These actions were condensed in the previous version

Lord God, heavenly King,
O God, almighty Father.

The Introductory Rites

- Entrance Procession and Chant ♪
- Greeting
- Penitential Act *or* blessing and sprinkling of water ♪
- Gloria ♪
- Collect (opening prayer).

The Opening Procession

- The order is as follows: server with thurible (if using incense); servers with candles, and between them the cross-bearer; other servers; a reader (or deacon) who may carry the Book of the Gospels; the priest celebrant.

- Occasionally other symbols may be processed in. These might highlight an aspect of the readings or the occasion/feast/time of the liturgical year. (If done, the processing of symbols takes place at this point of the Mass rather than during the Preparation of the Gifts.)

- If carrying incense, after the priest has venerated the altar with a kiss, the altar and people are incensed. The use of incense helps greatly to engage the senses in our worship.

- To unite us as one voice in song, the entrance hymn or chant is one we all know and that speaks of the season or action of the Mass.

A New Greeting

'And with your spirit' is the literal translation of what we find in the Latin text *et cum spiritu tuo*. This translation is already found in others languages, for example German, Italian, French and Spanish.

The source for this dialogue between priest and people is very much Scripture. In four letters of St Paul he uses the following greetings: Galatians 6:18 – May the grace of our Lord Jesus Christ be with your spirit; Philippians 4:23 – The grace of the Lord Jesus Christ be with your spirit; 2 Timothy 4:22 – The Lord be with your spirit; Philemon 13:25 – Grace be with all of you. Similar greetings can be found in the Old Testament.

Session Two

Christ Speaks to Us in the Scriptures Today

Structured Overview

Purpose of the Session

To explore the celebration and enactment of the Liturgy of the Word in the local context, bringing insights from the human, daily activity of hearing, listening and storytelling, from the scriptural encounter on the Emmaus journey and from the structure and presentation of the Liturgy of the Word in the Roman Missal. Once more, participants will be led to offer suggestions for local enhancement of the celebration of this part of the Mass.

Session Outline*

Welcome & Introductions
Opening Prayer . . . . (10 min)

Movement 1:
Paying attention to our own experience of listening and story-telling . . . . (10 min)

Movement 2:
Hearing the story and reflecting on the sharing of God's Word on
the journey to Emmaus . . . . (10 min)

Movement 3:
Applying the story to our own experience on a Sunday as a community . . (10 min)

Movement 4:
Exploring the liturgical action of the Liturgy of the Word on a Sunday . . . . (25 min)

Movement 5:
Making concrete suggestions for our own local experience . . . . (10 min)

Closing Prayer
Cuppa

(1 hr 15 min)

The time indicators are, once more, given as guides. From them, leaders can determine the time allocations they will give to each of the movements locally. Leaders might choose to run the session to 1 hr 30 min.

Checklist immediately prior to a session

- ☐ Set up the room in a warm and inviting manner, with chairs in a semi-circle rather than lecture style.
- ☐ Prepare a prayer focus in the room, for example a covered table with a candle, icon/cross, Bible.
- ☐ Have any technology needed ready for use before people arrive.
- ☐ Have any handouts/flip chart stand, paper and pens ready for use.
- ☐ Delegate any readings or other tasks to be done before the session begins.
- ☐ Welcome people as they arrive.

When the session begins
- ☐ Welcome people formally to the session. Welcome newcomers in particular to the programme.
- ☐ Introduce yourself and your role in the session.
- ☐ Introduce the session in the context of the programme 'Signposts on the Road to Emmaus' and the purpose of this second session.
- ☐ Remind people very briefly of the areas covered to date, namely the Introductory Rites of the Mass.
- ☐ Let people know the end time and whether or not a cup of tea/coffee is being offered at the end.
- ☐ Give people an opportunity to greet one another.
- ☐ Introduce the Opening Prayer – this can include the lighting of a candle.

Session Two: Christ Speaks to Us in the Scriptures Today

OPENING PRAYER

INVITATION TO PRAYER

We turn to our God once more in prayer, coming into God's presence and receiving God's life-giving word to us this day. In making the sign of faith upon our bodies, we open our whole selves to God as we pray in the name of the Father and of the Son and of the Holy Spirit. Amen.

*REFLECTION**

Deep
is where it is dark
where there is mystery
where the way is not known
where it is easy to become fearful
and even turn back.

but
Deep
within your heart,
God,
is where
there's always strength to go in
where truth becomes known
where your love holds me close
where I need not be afraid.

my hidden self,
Deep, Deep down
in the womb of Yourself:
safe
nourished
guarded
enlivened.

take me there, God.
I want to go.

SCRIPTURE

Your word is a lamp to my feet and a light to my path.

(PSALM 119:105)

You show me the path of life. In your presence there is fullness of joy.

(PSALM 16:11)

Then the word of the Lord came to him, saying '... Go out and stand on the mountain before the Lord, for the Lord is about to pass by.' Now there was a great wind, so strong that it was splitting mountains and breaking rocks in pieces before the Lord, but the Lord was not in the wind; and after the wind an earthquake, but the Lord was not in the earthquake; and after the earthquake a fire, but the Lord was not in the fire; and after the fire, a sound of sheer silence.
When Elijah heard it, he wrapped his face in his mantle and went out and stood at the entrance of the cave ...

(1 KINGS 19:9, 11:13)

---

* Taken from *Dear Heart, Come Home: The Path of Midlife Spirituality*, by Joyce Rupp (New York: Crossroad, 1996), p. 23.

This page may be photocopied

Quiet Moment
In the gift of the silence of this moment,
I welcome God's word to me.

Prayer
O Divine Word
You share your Truth with us each day.
Open our ears
that we may be attentive to the many ways you speak to us.
Open our hearts to receive your Truth
that we may come to fullness of life in You.
Open our minds
that the choices we make and the witness we give
will give glory to your name.
We ask this through Christ our Lord. Amen.

This page may be photocopied

SESSION TWO: CHRIST SPEAKS TO US IN THE SCRIPTURES TODAY

Movement 1 (10 min)
Paying attention to our experience of listening and story-telling

We begin by looking at the human experience of hearing in our daily lives. From the moment we awake until we go to bed our brain is bombarded by things demanding to be heard. In this quick exercise, participants are invited into an exploration of that daily activity of 'hearing', through which they hopefully will come to make subtle and not so subtle distinctions between things they hear and things to which they listen.

Leaders might draw upon *some* of the following questions as helpful. It is important to enter into this discussion with the awareness that there is a distinction between hearing and listening. To listen is to consciously make the active effort to truly hear what is being said.

> *Leader suggestion:* Record responses on a flip chart.

GROUP CONVERSATION
- What are the main things we hear?
- What are the main things we listen to? (Is there a difference?)
- Who do we listen to most willingly/least willingly?
- What/who do we hear that demands our attention?
- What do we hear that we can ignore/dismiss?
- Where/when do we listen best?
- Why do we listen to some people and not to others?

Another hugely important activity in our daily lives is that of storytelling.

- When do we share stories with one another? (*Answers might include coffee breaks, pub, mealtimes, outside school gates, at work, late at night, after Mass ...*)
- When do we share the significant stories of our lives – where, who, how?
- Why is it important to share our story?

Drawing the feedback together
The leader brings together what people have said, highlighting the main points that have emerged from the group.

Movement 2 (10 min)
Hearing the story and reflecting on the sharing of God's Word on the journey to Emmaus

> *Leader suggestion:* Before the session begins, have someone ready to read this Gospel passage, using a Bible.

At the first session we heard from the opening passage of the story of the two disciples on their journey to Emmaus and how they met Jesus along the road. We take up that story just after the disciples have expressed their surprise that the stranger does not appear to know about the events in Jerusalem.

Reading

A reading from the Holy Gospel according to Luke (24:19-27)

He asked them, 'What things?' They replied, 'The things about Jesus of Nazareth, who was a prophet mighty in deed and word before God and all the people, and how our chief priests and leaders handed him over to be condemned to death and crucified him. But we had hoped that he was the one to redeem Israel. Yes, and besides all this, it is now the third day since these things took place. Moreover, some women of our group astounded us. They were at the tomb early this morning, and when they did not find his body there, they came back and told us that they had indeed seen a vision of angels who said that he was alive. Some of those who were with us went to the tomb and found it just as the women had said; but they did not see him.' Then he said to them, 'Oh, how foolish you are, and how slow of heart to believe all that the prophets have declared! Was it not necessary that the Messiah should suffer these things and then enter into his glory?' Then beginning with Moses and all the prophets, he interpreted to them the things about himself in all the scriptures.

The Gospel of the Lord.

Reflection
This reflection, as is the case for all the reflections in this programme, can be done conversationally/interactively with the group. Leaders are invited to make the material their own.

We think again of those two travellers on the road, journeying from Jerusalem to Emmaus. How do you think that they were feeling? We are told sad, but probably also confused, shocked, perhaps angry. Angry at the authorities, at Jesus, at themselves and their own foolishness. Remember they are getting out of Jerusalem, heading back home. They had put their trust in this new prophet who was mighty in word and deed. But this mighty prophet, this one who was supposed to redeem Israel, ended up crucified like a common criminal. This is not how it was supposed to be.

And what do they go on to tell us? It's three days since his death, time has moved on and there seems to be no hope. They know of the empty tomb but fail to understand its meaning.

If they had really heard and listened to the prophets they would understand, but they haven't. Instead they have lived through the experience and have failed to grasp its meaning. And without this understanding, they fail to recognise the risen Lord in their presence.

Yet what does Jesus do? He takes the messengers of God's word, beginning with Moses and the prophets, and he unpacks their message for the travellers. Moreover, he explains to them how it all relates to Jesus. By doing so he is able to help the two travellers begin their journey to making sense of what they have just gone through in Jerusalem.

There are three steps here: **proclamation, interpretation, reception**, and we see these steps at play in our Mass every week.

Movement 3 (10 min)
Applying the story to our own experience on a Sunday as a community

Reflection

Let's reflect on that first step, the step of **Proclamation**. The word has to be spoken out loud; it then becomes real. We know that in life. We can go about for years with things unspoken – when said they become real, they become something we have to, get to, face and take on board. But we need prophets – people who will speak God's message to us. In our world we still have plenty of prophets. Every day we encounter God's prophets in our lives. We encounter people who knowingly or unknowingly speak a message of God to us. In our liturgy on a Sunday we also have our prophets. Who are they?

They are our Readers – those ministers of the liturgy who speak to us a message from God. They are the ones who say out loud the words of salvation. They utter into being God's words of love and healing. In the midst of the assembly they take their place and proclaim aloud our stories – stories that are not about buzzwords or the latest sound bites. These stories are about the lives of those who believe in and share in the promise of resurrection.

These stories, are not about what God did in the past but about what God is doing upon us now. We are told:

> When the sacred scriptures are read in the Church, God himself speaks to his people, and Christ, present in his own words, proclaims the Gospel. (*General Instruction of the Roman Missal*, 29)

In these stories, God speaks to us today and calls us into relationship with him, a relationship that brings us life in abundance, not mediocrity.

The reader articulates these stories in faith and through faith so that they can be received into the very being of those who have gathered.

But how do we interpret these words: we need to take the next step, that of **Interpretation**. On any given Sunday, the presence of Christ in the words of Scripture meets the presence of Christ in the very stuff of people's lives. We hear particular stories, particular messages in the context of a particular season in the Church year. If these are not to be mere sound bites, what difference do these words make? How do I receive these words into my life and shape my life as a result of them?

The task of the priest celebrant is to help us to do just that. He takes the proclaimed word and interprets it, hopefully, always in light of the resurrected Christ and in the context of the lives of the assembly who have gathered. His task is to help break open the word of God into the centre of our lives.

But no matter how rich the homily, how good the interpretation, at the end of the day the final step is up to us: **Reception**. This is because the journey from proclaimed word to interpreted word to lived word demands that the final action is ours. God gifts us with this word but ours is the initiative of response or non-response. Every day we make choices, take decisions, turn in particular directions, and act in particular ways.

The first choice that we are invited to make is to be authentic listeners of this proclaimed and interpreted word. And authentic listening can only result in a lived-out response.

But remember, Christ came that we might have life in abundance. Sometimes that life may not be what, where or when we expect it, but part of our listening to God is a listening to see God's word in action in our lives. Christ is present in the midst of the faithful through his word. It is our choice to welcome this presence into our lives and to allow God's word to speak to us in the rhythm of our lives.

We do this as individuals but we also do this as a community. This is why we can stand with one another in response to the word and profess our shared belief in the Creed. This is why we can offer our common petitions to God – asking for the needs of the whole world and not just ourselves.

Reflection Questions for the Group
» What helps our experience of sharing, hearing and receiving God's word at our weekend Mass?
» What hinders our experience?

> **Leader suggestion:** Depending on time, invite people to discuss the questions with a neighbour and then bring the questions to the large group or process. Chart responses if possible.

Movement 4 (30 min)
Exploring the liturgical action of the Liturgy of the Word on a Sunday

> *A timely reminder about our readings at Mass*
> The text read to us is not about handing on something that comes from the past, rather it is pointing to what God is doing here and now. (*Celebrating the Mystery of Faith*, National Centre for Liturgy, p. 73)

Over the course of a three-year cycle of Sunday readings, we listen to our story of salvation and redemption in the rhythm of the Church Year and in the rhythm of our lives.

Map out with people the journey of the Liturgy of the Word. Depending on the time available to you, you can ask people to call out the steps involved or present it straight through.

- First reading   *silence*
- Psalm ♪
- Second Reading   *silence*
- Gospel Acclamation ♪
- Gospel
- Homily   *silence*

- Profession of Faith/Creed
- Prayer of the Faithful/Universal Prayer ♪

LEADER BACKGROUND MATERIAL AND NOTES

The following notes can be drawn upon in walking through the Liturgy of the Word, explaining the different elements and offering suggestions for the enactment of this Rite in the local setting.

First Reading: This reading is usually from the Old Testament (though in the Easter season this reading will come from the Acts of the Apostles) and is typically chosen to link into the Gospel. When preparing the readings, it is helpful to examine all the readings of the day to see possible links.

> 'The word of the Lord'.
> Since the introduction of the new Missal, readers now conclude their reading with the statement of faith 'The word of the Lord' instead of 'This is the word of the Lord'. This is a direct translation from the Latin and is linked with similar statements of faith throughout the Mass, i.e. The Gospel of the Lord; The Mystery of Faith; The Body of Christ; The Blood of Christ.

Silence

A greater use of silence was called for in the revised *General Instruction of the Roman Missal*, published in English in 2005. Times of silence are explicitly indicated within the Missal itself, as can be demonstrated in the outline of the Liturgy of the Word above. The use of silence allows the readings to echo in the hearts of people.

Psalm

Psalms were written to be sung! Musicians and readers need to work together to ensure that the psalms can speak to God's people. The psalms are sometimes called the Christian prayerbook.

Second Reading

This reading is taken from the New Testament. In the strong seasons of Advent-Christmas and Lent-Easter it will normally link into the other two readings. In other seasons it may represent a semi-continuous reading of a particular book of the New Testament.

Silence

As above

Gospel Acclamation

This sung piece welcomes the Gospel that is about to be proclaimed. It calls us to a standing posture so that through our change in posture and our ritual use of music we are highlighting the Gospel as the highpoint of the Liturgy of the Word.

Gospel

The Risen Christ speaks to his people gathered today. We honour this word through our posture, gesture of signing ourselves, our use of incense and by our active listening to this sacred word to us.

Homily
The function of the homily is to literally break open the word that has been proclaimed into the life context of the community who has gathered.

Silence
The silence that follows the homily allows people to take on board what has been said, giving some precious moments for it to sit on their hearts.

Profession of Faith/Creed
Having heard and welcomed God's word, the community gives its assent and proclaims its faith in this prayer. Some of the changes in this text are highlighted in the handout with this session.

> *Leader suggestion:* Again leaders can decide whether to talk through the additional material on the Creed with participants or refer people to the handout for personal reading outside of the session.

> *The Nicene Creed – highlighting just some of the changes*
> The new translation aims to reflect the original Latin text more faithfully. This prayer professes the faith of Catholics each Sunday across the world. It is important that we say the same words.
> *'I believe'* While the Creed professes the faith of the entire Church, the use of 'I' in this prayer invites us to stand and assert individually our personal faith alongside that of other believers.
> *'Of all things visible and invisible'* This new wording adds precision to the previous translation. Something can be unseen (old translation) to you but this does not mean it is invisible – for example, a galaxy or tiny sea creature. God is the creator of all things – visible and invisible – for example, the saints and angels.
> *'Consubstantial with the Father'* is an example of a re-introduction of a theological term that will be unfamiliar to many people. What does it mean? The early Church leaders used the Greek term *homoousios* to express the belief that Jesus is of the same essential being and substance as the Father, even though they are separate and distinct persons. It reminds us that even though Jesus became a man he was also God. The Latin term is *consubstantialis*, giving us the word 'consubstantial'.
> *'Incarnate'* again reintroduces a time-honoured word that may be unfamiliar to many today. The birth of Jesus has significance beyond that of any other human birth. The Word became flesh in the womb of Mary, the Son of God *was* incarnate, assumed human nature.

Prayer of the Faithful/Universal Prayer
'The joy and hope, the struggle and anguish of the people of this age and especially the poor and those suffering in any way are the joy, and hope, the struggle and anguish of Christ's disciples.' (Vatican II)

Both the priest's introduction and the proposed intention are addressed to the congregation, not to God. They are invitations to the faithful, who then pray for the suggested intention in the silence of their hearts and in a common petition. Hence the need for silence within these intercessions. As a community we remember and pray for the needs of humankind. Just as our God is a lavish God, so too is our prayer. While we bring our own concerns before God, our prayer is expansive, moving out to include the needs of the whole world. In this sense our prayer is a 'universal prayer'. Indeed the Missal offers this as an alternative title for this set of prayers, together with Bidding Prayers. A sung response to these prayer petitions can strengthen the unity of our intercession to God.

Posture within the Liturgy of the Word

We sit to listen to the Lord who is our one true teacher. We stand in the presence of the Gospel, as we give our assent to these words of life. We sit for the Homily, as the presider applies these saving words to our life as a community, and we stand once more to proclaim our faith and pray for all creation in the Prayer of the Faithful. *(Celebrating the Mystery of Faith*, National Centre for Liturgy, p. 73.)

Some suggestions to focus on for the celebration of the Liturgy of the Word

Within the Rite:
- **Pace:** Allow one rite to finish and another to start. The reader comes forward once people have said the Amen of the Opening Prayer. Within the readings themselves, allow one piece of proclamation to settle on the people before moving to the next piece.
- **Sing** what can be sung! Music can be used for the Psalm, Gospel acclamation and the response to the Prayer of the Faithful.
- Highlight the importance and the Good News of the Gospel through the use of a **Gospel procession** with the singing of the acclamation, carrying of candles and the processing of the Book of the Gospels, if used, as well as the incensing of the book before the text is proclaimed.
- Consider the **Prayer of the Faithful.** Do they speak to the local and beyond, do they find inspiration from the word of God and from the events of the world? Pattern of each prayer – *announcement of the intention, silent prayer, response.* Models are provided in the Roman Missal. These prayers are an expression of our care and concern for the world in which we live.
- Use of **silence** throughout the rite – can be built up over a period of time.
- Use a **Lectionary** rather than proclaiming from a Missalette.

Movement 5 (10 min or to end)
Making concrete suggestions for our own local experience

Leader suggestion: Make sure to record in some way what people say and bring those findings to an appropriate forum for action.

» In light of what we have explored tonight, are there one or two things you would like to affirm in what you are doing as a worship community/parish?
» Are there one or two things you might suggest that you would like to see tried in the worship community/parish in the coming months?
» If time allows, have participants chat about the above for a few minutes with a neighbour and then hear from the wider group. Otherwise process the questions with the group immediately.
» Let people know that you will pass on what has been recommended to the local parish for the awareness of those who prepare the liturgy.

Depending on what comes from the group, leaders might note some of the following with the group or check how strongly the group feels about some of them.

Ongoing considerations for the worship community
- Draw upon diversity of ministers – readers, cantor, deacon, choir, homilist
- Formation and training of new and existing readers
- Preparation skills and resources for readers
- Sound system in church
- Homily – breaking open the Word into the lives of the people (being fed by a local Sunday reading reflection group?)
- The need or otherwise for a Liturgy of the Word appropriate for children. The starting point of any such exploration is that this is the children's and adult leader's **worship** and not Sunday school
- Our readiness to hear the word: putting next Sunday's readings or the citations for them in a bulletin.

WRAP-UP & CLOSING PRAYER

LEADER NOTE: CHECKLIST FOR CLOSE OF SESSION
- ☐ Remind people of what they have explored in the session
- ☐ Thank people for giving of their time and themselves in the session
- ☐ Let participants know when the next session of 'Signposts on the Road to Emmaus' will be taking place
- ☐ Announce what the focus of the next session will be: the celebration of the Liturgy of the Eucharist, beginning with the Preparation of the Gifts and exploring up as far as the Great Amen
- ☐ Invite people to stay for a cup of tea/coffee where applicable
- ☐ Lead or invite another to bring the session to a close with a final prayer.

CLOSING PRAYER
God of Wisdom,
We know that your Word has become flesh and lives amongst us.

> Let us hold this Word constantly in our hearts.
> Let us be open to your voice speaking to us.
> Let us know how to stand before you in silence.

May we be faithful hearers of your Word
and doers of your Word in our lives.

We ask this in the name of Christ our Lord. Amen.

Further Reading:

National Centre for Liturgy, *Celebrating the Mystery of Faith* (Dublin: Veritas, 2011)

National Centre for Liturgy, *The New Missal: Explaining the Changes* (Dublin: Veritas, 2011)

International Eucharistic Congress 2012, *The Eucharist: Communion With Christ and With One Another: Theological and Pastoral Reflections in Preparation for the 50th International Eucharistic Congress* (Dublin: Veritas, 2011)

Session Two Handout

Christ Speaks to Us in the Scriptures Today

> *When the sacred scriptures are read in the Church, God himself speaks to his people, and Christ, present in his own words, proclaims the Gospel.* (General Instruction of the Roman Missal, 29)
>
> *The text read to us is not about handing on something that comes from the past, rather it is pointing to what God is doing here and now.* (Celebrating the Mystery of Faith, p. 73)

Postures within the Liturgy of the Word

'We sit to listen to the Lord who is our one true teacher. We stand in the presence of the Gospel, as we give our assent to these words of life. We sit for the homily, as the presider applies these saving words to our life as a community; and we stand once more to proclaim our faith and pray for all creation in the Prayer of the Faithful.' (*Celebrating the Mystery of Faith*, p. 73)

The Journey of the Liturgy of the Word

- First reading   *silence*
- Psalm ♪
- Second Reading   *silence*
- Gospel Acclamation ♪
- Gospel
- Homily   *silence*
- Profession of Faith/Creed
- Prayer of the Faithful ♪

This page may be photocopied

The Pattern of each prayer: announcement of the intention; silent prayer response.

A New Conclusion to the Readings: 'The word of the Lord'

With the introduction of the new Missal, readers will now conclude their reading with the statement of faith 'The word of the Lord' instead of 'This is the word of the Lord'. This is a direct translation from the Latin and is linked with similar statements of faith throughout the Mass, i.e. The Gospel of the Lord, The Mystery of Faith, The Body of Christ, The Blood of Christ.

Some Suggestions for Celebrating the Liturgy of the Word

- **Pace:** Allow one rite to finish and another to start. The reader comes forward once people have said the Amen of the Opening Prayer. Within the readings themselves, allow one piece of proclamation to settle on the people before moving to the next piece.
- **Sing** what can be sung! Music can be used for the Psalm, Gospel acclamation and the response to the Prayer of the Faithful.
- Highlight the importance and the Good News of the Gospel through the use of a **Gospel procession** with the singing of the acclamation, a carrying of candles and the processing of the Book of the Gospels, if used, as well as the incensing of the book before the text is proclaimed.
- Consider the **Prayer of the Faithful**. Do they speak to the local and beyond, do they find inspiration from the word of God and from the events of the world? These prayers are an expression of our care and concern for the world in which we live.
- Use of **silence** throughout the rite – can be built up over a period of time.
- Use a **Lectionary** rather than proclaiming from a Missalette.

Prayer of the Faithful/ Universal Prayer

'The joy and hope, the struggle and anguish of the people of this age and especially the poor and those suffering in any way are the joy, and hope, the struggle and anguish of Christ's disciples.' (Vatican II)

Both the priest's introduction and the proposed intention are addressed to the congregation, not to God. They are invitations to the faithful, who then pray for the suggested intention in the silence of their hearts and in a common petition. Hence the need for silence within these intercessions.

The Nicene Creed – highlighting some of the changes

The new translation aims to reflect the original Latin text more faithfully. This prayer professes the faith of Catholics each Sunday across the world. It is important that we say the same words.

'I believe' While the Creed professes the faith of the entire Church, the use of 'I' in this prayer invites us to stand and assert individually our personal faith alongside that of other believers.

'Of all things visible and invisible' This new wording adds precision to the previous translation. Something can be unseen (old translation) to you but this does not mean it is invisible; for example, a galaxy or tiny sea creature. God is the creator of all things – visible and invisible, for example the saints and angels.

'Consubstantial with the Father' is an example of a re-introduction of a theological term that will be unfamiliar to many people. What does it mean? The early Church leaders used the Greek term *homoousios* to express the belief that Jesus is of the same essential being and substance as the Father, even though they are separate and distinct persons. It reminds us that even though Jesus became a man he was also God. The Latin term is *consubstantialis*, giving us the word 'consubstantial'.

'Incarnate' again reintroduces a time-honoured word that may be unfamiliar to many today. The birth of Jesus has significance beyond that of any other human birth. The Word become flesh in the womb of Mary, the Son of God was incarnate, assumed human nature.

In the year ahead, why not ...

- Consider regularly using a Gospel Procession using the Book of the Gospels with candles and incense
- Work with readers to find out and respond to their needs
- Encourage scripture reflection
- Explore how the singing of the Psalm can become more common
- Nurture silence within the Liturgy of the Word.

Session Three

Christ is Our Host

Structured Overview

Purpose of the Session

To explore the celebration and enactment of the Liturgy of the Eucharist, from the Preparation of the Gifts to the Great Amen. The session will highlight the dynamic and transforming power of meal-sharing and giving thanks to God in our life and in the Eucharist. The insights gained will come from the human experience of meals and meal-sharing, reflecting upon the meal at Emmaus and the Liturgy of the Eucharist itself as given to us in the texts of the Roman Missal. This will lead to practical suggestions for the local enrichment of the celebration of the Liturgy of the Eucharist.

Session Outline*

Welcome & Introductions
Opening Prayer . . . . (10 min)

Movement 1:
Paying attention to our own experience of sharing significant meals . . . . . . (7 min)

Movement 2:
Hearing the story and reflecting on the meal shared at Emmaus. . . . . (7 min)

Movement 3:
Applying the story to our own experience on a Sunday as a community . . . (10 min)

Movement 4:
Exploring the Preparation of the Gifts and the Eucharistic Prayer. . . . . . . (30 min)

Movement 5:
Making concrete suggestions for our own local experience . . . . (10 min)

Closing Prayer
Cuppa

(1hr 14min)

The time indicators are, once more, given as guides. From them, leaders can determine the time allocations they will give to each of the movements locally. Leaders might choose to run the session to 1 hr and 30 min.

Checklist immediately prior to a session
- ☐ Set up the room in a warm and inviting manner, with chairs in a semi-circle rather than lecture style.
- ☐ Prepare a prayer focus in the room, for example a covered table with a candle, icon/cross, Bible. Bread, grapes, wheat and a chalice might also be used.
- ☐ Have any technology needed ready for use before people arrive.
- ☐ Have any handouts/flip chart stand, paper and pens ready for use.
- ☐ Delegate any readings or other tasks to be done before the session begins.
- ☐ Welcome people as they arrive.

When the session begins
- ☐ Welcome people formally to the session. Welcome newcomers in particular to the programme.
- ☐ Introduce yourself and your role in the session.
- ☐ Introduce the session in the context of the programme 'Signposts on the Road to Emmaus' and the purpose of this third session.
- ☐ Remind people very briefly of the areas covered to date, namely the Introductory Rites of the Mass and the Liturgy of the Word.
- ☐ Let people know the end time and whether or not a cup of tea/coffee is being offered at the end.
- ☐ Give people an opportunity to greet one another.
- ☐ Introduce the Opening Prayer – this can include the lighting of a candle.

SESSION THREE: CHRIST IS OUR HOST

OPENING PRAYER

INVITATION TO PRAYER

As we gather to explore and deepen our understanding of the Mass, we turn in a spirit of prayer and thanksgiving to our God who blessed us with the gift of creation and who continues to bless us in our lives. As we make the sign of the cross over our bodies, we are conscious that all we are and all we have comes from God our Creator. In the name of the Father and of the Son and of the Holy Spirit. Amen.

SCRIPTURE

Lord our God,
the whole world tells
the greatness of your name.
Your glory reaches beyond the stars.

I see your handiwork
in the heavens:
The moon and the stars
You set in place.

What is humankind
that you remember them,
the human race
that you care for them?

You give them charge of the earth,
laying all at their feet:

Cattle and sheep,
Wild beasts,
Birds of the sky,
Fish of the sea,
Every swimming creature.

Lord our God
the whole world tells
the greatness of your name.

(Psalm 8:2, 4-5, 7-10)*

REFLECTION

'Winter Wheat'**

She said, 'Well, you seed it in September. And it comes up right away. Then it dies back down and you hope for a good snow cover. If there's been enough moisture it comes back up in April, around Easter.'

QUIET MOMENT

In a moment of quiet we reflect on how we each, in our own individual way, share in the work of God's creation.

LITANY

Loving God, the wonder of your creation surrounds us daily, calling us to recognise the beauty of your handiwork in our lives. We thank you for your eternal presence.
R. Blessed be God for ever.

---

* *From a translation prepared by the International Commission on English in the Liturgy.*
** Taken from *Dakota: A Spiritual Geography*, by Kathleen Norris (New York: Ticknor & Fields, 1993), p. 188.

This page may be photocopied

God of gentleness, the delicacy and fragility of your creation calls us to ways of care and protection of the world. We dedicate ourselves to care for your creation.
R. Blessed be God for ever.

God of wisdom, what you have created has been entrusted to us in stewardship. We offer our gifts, our talents, and our time to enhance the gift of creation that you have bestowed upon us.
R. Blessed be God for ever.

God of all ages, in Christ you gave us the greatest gift, the gift of yourself. In the Eucharist we remember this awesome gift that feeds all our hunger.
R. Blessed be God for ever.

Prayer
'Beginners'*
We have only begun to imagine the fullness of life,
How could we tire of hope?
So much is in bud,
So much is unfolding that must complete its gesture,
So much is in bud.

Glory be to the Father, and to the Son, and to the Holy Spirit. As it was in the beginning, is now and ever shall be, world without end. Amen.

---

* Taken from *Cries of the Spirit: A Celebration of Women's Spirituality*, edited by Marilyn Sewell (Boston: Beacon Press, 1991), pp. 181–2.

This page may be photocopied

SESSION THREE: CHRIST IS OUR HOST

Movement 1 (7 min)
Paying attention to our experience of sharing significant meals

In the course of our life we share many meals. Many of these meals are perfunctory, necessary to sustain us through our day. Some of these meals emerge as far more significant than others. In this quick exercise, leaders can help participants to process what stands out about significant meals that they have shared with others in their life.
Draw upon some of the following questions as helpful.

> **Leader suggestion:** If possible, chart the findings for referencing within the session.

GROUP CONVERSATION
Draw upon some of the following questions as helpful.
- » Think of some the important meals that you have experienced in your life. What made them different to other meals?
- » As a host, how do you go about preparing for an important meal?
- » As a guest, how do you go about preparing for an important meal?
- » Do good experiences of meals have any similar patterns or elements to them?

Drawing the feedback together
Having processed the questions with the group, the leader reminds participants what they have collectively expressed as key learning about sharing meals.

Movement 2 (7 min)
Hearing the story and reflecting on the meal shared at Emmaus

> **Leader suggestion:** Before the session begins, have someone ready to read this Gospel passage, using a Bible.

In the first two sessions of 'Signposts on the Road to Emmaus', we heard from the opening passage of the story of the two disciples on their journey to Emmaus and how they met Jesus along the road. We heard how Jesus broke open their experience for them through the Word of God, beginning with Moses and the Prophets, and how the writings of the Old Testament related to Jesus himself. We take up that story just as Jesus makes to leave them.

READING

A reading from the Holy Gospel according to Luke (24:28-32)

As they came near the village to which they were going, he walked ahead as if he were going on. But they urged him strongly, saying, 'Stay with us, because it is almost evening and the day is now nearly over.' So he went in to stay with them. When he was at the table with them, he took bread, blessed and broke it, and gave it to them. Then their eyes were opened, and they recognised him; and he vanished from their sight. They said to each other, 'Were not our hearts burning within us while he was talking to us on the road, while he was opening the scriptures to us?'

The Gospel of the Lord.

REFLECTION
This reflection, as is the case for all the reflections in this programme, can be done conversationally/interactively with the group. Leaders are invited to make the material their own.

Once more we see in this Gospel passage an action that is at the heart of our liturgy and our ministry: an action of hospitality and welcome. We have Jesus making as if to leave (though clearly he had no intention of doing so) and the two urge him to stay with them. They urge him not just to stay, but to stay *with* them, stay in this relationship.

We see here a very human impulse at work, the impulse to stay with something good, to prolong the good experience. We see the natural impulse to want to continue in an experience in which we find nourishment. They have been fed by word and now, aware of their hunger for more, they will be fed by bread.

And in this story we see a very simple but significant reversal in roles. Christ moves from being the guest to being the host. The two invite him to dine with them. They provide the setting and the provisions for the meal. But Christ is clearly the host of the meal. And it is Christ who leads the eucharistic actions of taking, blessing, breaking and sharing.

Think of the image of meal and bread at the heart of this encounter. There is something deeply intimate about the sharing of food. Food is fraught with images of companionship, community, sharing, feast, giving of self. Food and drink becomes part of who you are – you are what you eat!

(At this point, if helpful, you might refer back to what emerged in the group questions at the beginning of the session.)

Bread itself is the staff of life. It sustains us. It represents our basic, daily nourishment. But it also represents the gift of God's creation and our participation in God's work – 'fruit of the earth and work of human hands'. As the land yields its harvest we give of ourselves and of our labour in the fashioning of bread from the grains of wheat.

For a moment let's turn our attention back to these travelling companions. They quite literally, as companions, broke bread together in their shared meal. In that human interaction we find hospitality, fellowship, nourishment, thanksgiving. In the intimacy of a meal, in the taking, blessing, breaking and sharing of bread, they recognise for the first time who is in their midst – *they recognise Christ and the ongoing gift of Christ's sacrifice.*

So they recognise Christ and what happens? He vanishes. In the moment they recognise him, he is gone. They move from a real presence to a seeming absence in an instant. But that seeming absence, that emptiness now has a totally new meaning and content, for now that emptiness is full of Christ's presence.

So the two disciples don't panic. They don't call out for Christ to come back; they don't despair. Rather they remember and they continue to recognise. They look back and they remember and recognise the burning of their hearts as Christ had unpacked God's word for them; they recognise Christ in the stranger who had walked with them; they recognise now the abiding presence of Christ despite his apparent absence.

Having walked with Christ, having listened to his Word and shared in his meal, these two disciples believe and know that Christ is indeed present – even where there appears to be absence.

Movement 3 (10 min)
Applying the story to our own experience on a Sunday as a community

Again the following reflection can be done conversationally with the group.

Reflection
On a Sunday we get to follow in the footsteps of these two travellers on the road. We come with our own hungers to the celebration of Mass and with some confidence that our hunger can be fed in this celebration – 'Give us this day our daily bread ...' is a petition not just for physical but for spiritual nourishment.

And just like our two friends at Emmaus, once our liturgy begins it is Christ who is our host. We as a community get to prepare our worship, to set the scene, but it is Christ who prays in us and who leads our prayer.

We see unfolding before us in our liturgy the similar pattern of taking, blessing, breaking and sharing bread. We saw it at the Last Supper; we also saw it at the feeding of the five thousand; and again at Emmaus. Indeed, at the Last Supper Christ instructed his followers to follow this pattern, in memory of him. In this session we will focus on the first two steps of this pattern, looking the next time at the subsequent ones.

We get to bring the gifts of bread and also wine to the table, to the altar of the Lord. We, the people of God, the community of the faithful, present this bread and wine for transformation into the Body and Blood of Christ. But in so doing we also present ourselves. As this bread and wine (the gifts of God's creation and our participation in the work of God – 'fruit of the earth and work of human hands') will be changed through the work of the Spirit, so too we will be transformed. This is one of the many gifts of the Eucharist. Again and again we can bring ourselves to God so that God's love and graciousness can work upon us.

In the second step of this pattern we find our great prayer of thanksgiving – the Eucharistic Prayer. Following in the tradition and invitation of Jesus, we give thanks and bless God for all that God has done for us. This is the heart of our celebration. By recalling the great deeds that God has done in the past we pray that God will continue to do them in the present. This is central to what we mean by 'memorial'.

By recalling what is central to our faith – the death and resurrection of Jesus – Christ makes present to us anew the sacrifice offered 'once for all' on Golgotha. *The memorial of the Mass makes present and effective in the here and now an event in the past.* The memorial of the Mass is the ongoing pouring out and sharing of the gift of the self-giving love of God in Christ.

In the Eucharistic Prayer, in this great prayer of the Church, we unite in thanksgiving and in reverence at the great gift we receive in God-made-flesh. Through this prayer and its actions, our humble gifts of bread and wine will return to us transformed into the extraordinary gift of the Body and Blood of Christ.

Reflection Questions for the Group
Having looked at the significance of 'meal' in the opening group exercise, the following offers an opportunity to focus on the element of thanksgiving which is central to Eucharist. Indeed, this might be a good time to note for participants that the word 'Eucharist' itself means 'to give thanks'. As people who celebrate the Eucharist we are invited to look at the gift of our lives from a starting point of gratitude and thanks.

These reflection questions, then, do not directly relate to the reflection preceding it but rather seek to move participants forward, deeper into the exploration of Eucharist.

» What have we to be thankful for?
» How do we live our thanksgiving?

> *Leader suggestion:* Discuss the questions above as one group and chart the feedback.

Movement 4 (30 min)
Exploring the Preparation of the Gifts and the Eucharistic Prayer

Because of the amount of material involved, the Liturgy of the Eucharist is explored over two sessions. In this session we look at the Preparation of the Gifts and the Eucharistic Prayer. The next session will include an exploration of the Communion Rite.

> At the Last Supper, Christ instituted the Paschal Sacrifice and banquet, by which the Sacrifice of the Cross is continuously made present in the Church. From the days of the apostles the Church has celebrated that sacrifice by carrying out what the Lord himself did and handed over to his disciples to be done in his memory.
>
> Like him, it has *taken* bread and wine, *given thanks* to God over them, *broken* the bread, and *shared* the bread and cup of blessing as the Body and Blood of Christ. (*Celebrating the Mystery of Faith*, p. 53.)
>
> The four actions of the Liturgy of the Eucharist – **taking, blessing, breaking, sharing**.

Journey of the Liturgy of the Eucharist
Map out with people in broad strokes the journey of the Liturgy of the Eucharist. Depending on time you can ask people to call out the steps or present it straight through

> - Preparation of the gifts ... ***Take***
> - The Eucharistic Prayer ... ***Bless***
> - The Communion Rite (to be explored next time) ... ***Break and Share***

The following input has two foci: Part 1) the preparation of the gifts (15 min); and Part 2) the Eucharistic Prayer (15 min). Explore with participants these parts of the Mass, in turn drawing where appropriate on the following notes.

Part 1: The Preparation of the Gifts

The **purpose** of this rite is to make the altar, the gifts that are placed on it and the congregation ready for the Eucharistic offering that is to follow. Our attention shifts from the table of the Word to the table of the Altar.

During this preparation rite the congregation **sits** and watches the unfolding action, joining in the accompanying hymn if appropriate and readying themselves to enter into the next phase of the celebration of the Mass.

Order of Rite
- The Altar is dressed with corporal and Missal
- The collection of money and/or other gifts takes place
- The gifts of bread, wine and charity are presented by the people
- The priest says a blessing over the gifts, inaudibly if there is music. If there is no music he may say the blessing audibly, in which case the people respond 'Blessed be God for ever'
- The gifts, altar, cross, priest and people may be incensed
- The priest washes his hands – a ritual gesture of cleansing
- Invitation to people with response. 'Pray brothers and sisters ...' to which the people stand to respond
- Prayer over the offering.

Leader Background Material and Notes

The above order can be unpacked, again in a conversational and engaging style, with participants. To help leaders do this, the following notes are given as background material. They can be used as appropriate with the group in walking through the order of the rite.

The altar is first dressed to receive the gifts by placing a corporal (a white cloth) and Missal on it, as well as purificators (smaller white cloths for use with any chalices).

The gifts: It is one of the Church's most ancient customs that the people themselves provided the materials for the Eucharist. Historically, they also brought other foodstuffs to be blessed for their own use and for the poor. In this bringing of the gifts of bread and wine by the people themselves, we are underscoring our participation in the work of the liturgy. We are aligning ourselves with the action of the Mass. At this point we are invited to not only offer these gifts of the earth but also the gift of our very selves. We bring ourselves to the table of the Lord for transformation.

The **collection of money** takes place first, after the Prayer of the Faithful. This is not an interruption to the liturgy but is rather a profound reminder to us of the central call to Christian charity that has endured in the Church. Its purpose and value will therefore be better appreciated if, after the Prayer of the Faithful, the priest and people all sit and wait while the collection is taken and then made ready with the other gifts for the procession.

When ready, the **gifts of bread, wine and money are then carried forward** by members of the congregation. The gifts are accepted by the priest and are placed on the altar with a prescribed formula to which we reply, only when they are said out loud, *Blessed be God forever.* (This prayer formula is based on a particular Jewish model of blessing prayer.)

Before saying the prayer over the chalice containing wine, the priest pours the wine and some water into the chalice – the combination of water and wine being a sign of the divinity and humanity of Christ.

Ideally, **enough bread** should be brought forward to facilitate as many people as possible to receive hosts consecrated at this Mass (as is called for in the Missal). This demands preparation and management but underscores the liturgy as a living action of today, of this congregation, of this assembly of faith. We also look forward to the *Lamb of God* when we break down the consecrated host in order to share it – the idea of one bread broken down and shared so that we can become whole. This suggests bringing forward at least some hosts large enough to be broken down when the time comes.

♪ *Music ministers can support the action of this rite with the appropriate choice of music. When music is used the prayers of the priest are said inaudibly, up to the invitation 'Pray brothers and sisters …'.*

After the blessing prayers, the gifts, the cross and the altar may be **incensed**. If another minister is present (i.e. a deacon or server) the priest and people may also be incensed or the priest may incense the people.

The Missal says the following about this action:

> 'The priest may incense the gifts placed on the altar and then incense the cross and the altar itself, so as to signify the Church's offering and prayer rising like incense in the sight of God. Next, the priest, because of his sacred ministry, and the people, by reason of their baptismal dignity, may be incensed by the deacon or another minister.' (*General Instruction of the Roman Missal*, 75)

The priest then washes his hands. This is a ritual action rather than an action of hygiene, said with the ritual words, 'Wash me, O Lord, from my iniquity and cleanse me from my sin.'

The Prayer over the Offerings
The Prayer over the Offerings concludes this preparation rite for the Eucharistic prayer. It begins with an invitation to pray and a people's response. We find just one change in the new Missal to both the Priest's invitation and our response:

Priest: Pray brethren (brothers and sisters) that **my sacrifice and yours** may be acceptable to God, the almighty Father.
*To which we **stand** and reply*: May the Lord accept the sacrifice at your hands for the praise and glory of his name, for our good and the good of all his **holy** Church.

The priest's words should not be interpreted as referring to two separate sacrifices but rather is a reference to the ordained minister and the lay faithful united in one act of worship.

The Prayer over the Offerings then follows. This prayer is similar to the Collect and the Prayer after Communion in that its text changes from celebration to celebration.

> *Suggestions for Parish Practice:*
> - Have the collection at this time, with enough collectors for it to be carried out promptly
> - Have the gifts of bread and wine and the monetary gifts brought forward to the altar from the people
> - Bring forward enough hosts to be consecrated and shared with at least a sizeable proportion of the people who have gathered for this Mass
> - Present some hosts that can be broken down to be shared at the *Lamb of God*
> - Music – suitable sung or instrumental, or occasionally, silence
> - Enrich this rite with the use of incense
> - Move to a standing posture in readiness for the Eucharistic Prayer.

PART 2: THE EUCHARISTIC PRAYER
The Eucharistic Prayer begins with the opening dialogue and concludes with the Amen to the Doxology. In our new Missal we now have a richer fare of Eucharistic prayers to choose from. These are:
- Eucharistic Prayers I, II, III & IV
- Two Eucharistic Prayers for Reconciliation
- Eucharistic Prayer for Use in Masses for Various Needs (including four different forms).

There are also three Children's Eucharistic Prayers that are not contained in the Missal but that can still be used at Masses at which children are the primary group present.

While some of the texts of the Eucharistic Prayers will vary, every Eucharistic prayer includes the following elements:

> ***Leader suggestion:*** Give participants a copy of Eucharistic Prayer II at this point to help them identify the different parts of the prayer as outlined (you will find it on p. 93).

- Opening Dialogue ♪
- Preface
- Acclamation – Holy Holy … ♪
- Invocation of the Holy Spirit
- Institution Narrative and Consecration
- Memorial Acclamation ♪
- Memorial of the Paschal Mystery and Offering
- Intercessions
- Concluding Doxology with Amen ♪

The chief elements of this prayer are *thanksgiving, remembrance, praise* and *intercession*.

Through all the actions, symbols, gestures and words of this great prayer of the Church, we receive back our humble gifts of bread and wine beyond our imagination as the Body and Blood of Christ.

Leader Background Material and Notes

Leaders can draw upon the following notes as appropriate to walk through the above structure and content of the Eucharist prayer. It is offered as supporting reading *but leaders should only take from it what they need.*

Opening Dialogue

In this dialogue the priest invites us to lift our hearts towards the Lord in prayer and thanksgiving. Just as we have done with our bodies, our hearts are called to rise up to the Lord.

In the new Missal, as well as the consistent response to 'The Lord be with you', we find one other change in this dialogue, which at first glance may appear quite abrupt in comparison to what we had before:

'Let us give thanks to the Lord our God', now has the response 'It is right and just'. This again is a direct translation of what is in the Latin text.

Within this dialogue at the very opening of our great prayer we find something very important at work. There is an underscoring here of priest and people praying this prayer together. The priest draws all of us into what is to follow. He addresses the Eucharistic Prayer to the Father in the name of the entire community. This is an important point not to be missed.

Indeed when we respond 'It is right and just', we find these words coming back to us immediately in how the priest takes these words and uses them to move into the text of the Preface when he prays: 'It is right and just, our duty and our salvation ...' It is almost like he is saying to us, 'You are right, it is right and just and this is why it is so!' In the Preface we remember the many good reasons for our attitude of thanksgiving (*eucharistia* – the giving of thanks – Eucharist) before God.

♪ *The shared pattern of word and phrasing as required in sung texts gives added strength to our unity as we enter into this great prayer of the Church. Congregations will benefit by choosing to sing this exchange between priest celebrant and people.*

Preface

In this opening phase of the prayer, we recount the good deeds of God and give thanks to God for the whole work of salvation. There are many prefaces to choose from depending on the feast and occasion. Indeed, on a given feast day it can be very helpful to look to the preface for a deeper understanding of the feast being celebrated.

- Eucharistic Prayer IV and the Eucharistic Prayers for Use in Masses for Various Needs each have their own preface, which is used whenever that prayer is prayed
- Eucharistic Prayer II has its own preface but it may also be used with other prefaces
- Eucharistic Prayers for Reconciliation I and II both have their own prefaces but can also be used with a penitential preface
- Eucharistic Prayer I and III do not have their own preface.

Holy, Holy (Sanctus) ♪

In this great hymn (hence we more appropriately sing it!) we have a moment in the liturgy when the prayer of heaven and of earth is very explicitly united. Using scripture texts from both Isaiah 6:3 ('And one called to another and said: "Holy, holy, holy is the LORD of hosts; the whole earth is full of his glory"') and Matthew 21:9 ('The crowds that went ahead of him and that followed were shouting, "Hosanna to the Son of David! Blessed is the one who comes in the name of the Lord! Hosanna in the highest heaven!"'), we join with the saints and the heavenly hosts of angels.

In the new translation we find just one change with the use of 'hosts' rather than 'power and might'. The use of the word 'hosts' is a translation of *Sabaoth*, which is a Hebrew word found in the Latin text. It refers to the heavenly hosts of angels. Think of those heavenly hosts we sing of in the second verse of 'Silent Night'.

At the end of the Holy, Holy, the congregation **kneels** in reverence as we enter deeper into the Eucharistic Prayer.

Invocation of the Holy Spirit (or Epiclesis)

In every sacrament, whether it is baptism, marriage, Eucharist or any of the other sacraments, at some point we find an invocation to God to send the Holy Spirit. In all our Eucharistic prayers the Church petitions God to send down the Spirit upon the gifts of bread and wine so that they might become the Body and Blood of Christ. In many of our Eucharistic Prayers we find a further invocation to send the Holy Spirit upon the gathered community so that they may become one in the Body of Christ.

Institution Narrative and Consecration

'The words of Jesus, in which he gave himself to his disciples as their food and drink, are now repeated in the context of this prayer of praise. In the power of the Spirit, these words achieve what they promise and express: the presence of Christ and his Sacrifice among his people assembled.' (*Celebrating the Mass*, Bishops' Conference of England and Wales, 194)

> *Leader suggestion:* People might be invited to refer to the handout for take-home reading if time does not allow for the following.

Changes to this text in the new Missal

We note five changes in particular:

1. In the words over the bread we find a slight change in 'Eat *of* it'. The purpose of this is to make reference to the fact that we, though many, share in the one bread. Therefore we eat *of* this one bread, rather than implying an individual consuming of it in its entirety
2. The word 'chalice' replaces the word 'cup'. This word, found in the Latin text, was already in the Irish-language version. It is suggestive of a sacred vessel from which more than one person can drink
3. 'Eternal' replaces the word 'everlasting'. 'Eternal' is found in the Latin text and is a word outside the measure of time, whereas 'everlasting' suggests lasting long in time.
4. 'Poured out' replaces 'shed'. This is to allow for the ambiguity of the text. Only blood is shed, whilst both blood and wine can be poured
5. The new translation also replaces the phrase 'for all' with the phrase 'for many'. This translates what is found in the Latin text, *pro multis*, and is also what is found in the accounts of the Last Supper in Mark and in Paul's Letter to the Corinthians. This is not intended to imply that God's love is limited or that Christ did not die on the cross for all men and women. Rather it acknowledges that human beings may choose whether or not to accept the gift of salvation. The Church's enduring teaching, however, continues to be that Christ's salvation is for all.

Memorial Acclamation ♪

As an acclamation of the people, this is intended as a sung text. This acclamation confesses the Church's belief in the central mystery of our faith – the Paschal Mystery of Christ's Death, Resurrection and Presence among his people.

The 1975 Missal gave us five acclamations, including *My Lord and My God*, which was included 'for Ireland only'. In the new edition of the Missal we find four acclamations.

The first acclamation is a new translation of the Latin text. This Latin text is what the first two acclamations in the previous Missal were both based on: a) *Christ has died* ... and b) *Dying you destroyed our death* ...

6. There is almost no change in the second acclamation *When we eat this Bread* ...
7. In the third, now beginning *Save us, Saviour of the world* ... there is a change to the word 'order'.
8. The acclamation *My Lord and My God* has been retained for use in Ireland.

Many will miss the familiar 'Christ has died' acclamation. This has not been retained because it is not an address **to** Christ but rather contains statements **about** Christ. Hopefully we will continue to sing it on other occasions, for example during the Stations of the Cross.

The invitation to the Memorial Acclamation has also changed, from 'Let us proclaim the Mystery of Faith' to the more direct 'The Mystery of Faith', echoing the pattern of faith statements that we find elsewhere in the liturgy: The Word of the Lord, The Body of Christ.

Memorial of the Paschal Mystery and Offering (or *Anamnesis* and Offering)

This element of the prayer continues on from the Memorial Acclamation. The Church, fulfilling the Lord's command, celebrates and recalls as a memorial to the Lord his Passion, Resurrection and Ascension into heaven. In this memorial, these saving deeds of God in Christ are effective here and now.

As a community of faith, we offer to God this 'once for all' sacrifice of Christ that brings salvation to the whole world. In doing so, as an assembly we also join ourselves to this offering.

Second Invocation of the Holy Spirit (or Epiclesis)

With the exception of Eucharistic Prayer I, a second epiclesis occurs at this stage of the prayer. Just as we offer the 'Bread of life' and the 'Chalice of blessing' (Eucharistic Prayer for Use in Masses for Various Needs) we too offer our very selves to God. We pray that God will send the Holy Spirit upon us. In paying attention to this prayer, we are reminded of the transformative power of the Eucharist upon the assembly itself – making of it 'one body, one spirit in Christ' (Eucharistic Prayer III).

Intercessions

The prayer goes on to pray that the fruits of the sacrifice of Christ may be experienced throughout the Church and the world in a series of intercessions. These intercessions deepen our bond with the saints and Mary, the local Church and the ministerial Church as well as those gone before us.

Doxology and Amen ♪

The Eucharistic Prayer concludes where it began, with a prayer of praise and glory to God. This prayer is endorsed by all present in their 'Amen'. This 'Amen' not only ratifies the prayer of the Doxology but also what has been prayed in the whole of the Eucharistic Prayer.

Again our Amen is intended to be sung. Musical settings that extend the Amen or repeat it can help the congregation to experience its power as we draw the Eucharistic Prayer to a close.

Some Parish Suggestions to focus on for the Eucharistic Prayer
- Explore the variety of Eucharistic Prayers available for use
- Explore singing more often as a community
- Sing the acclamations and the opening dialogue
- Posture of the assembly during this prayer – standing, then moving to kneeling
- Encourage families to pray before meals in the home and make the link between that prayer and the Mass.

Movement 5 (10 min or to end)
Making concrete suggestions for our own local experience

» Is there anything in particular that strikes you in what we have explored tonight?
» In light of our exploration tonight, are there one or two things you would like to affirm in what you are doing as a worshipping community?
» Are there one or two things you might suggest that you would like to see tried in the worshipping community in the coming months?

If time allows, have participants chat about the above for a few minutes with a neighbour and then hear from the wider group. Otherwise, process the questions with the group immediately. Let people know that you will pass on what has been recommended to the local parish for the awareness of those who prepare the liturgy.

WRAP-UP & CLOSING PRAYER

LEADER NOTE: CHECKLIST FOR CLOSE OF SESSION
- ☐ Remind people of what they have explored in the session
- ☐ Thank people for giving of their time and themselves in the session
- ☐ Let participants know when the next session of 'Signposts on the Road to Emmaus' will be taking place
- ☐ Announce what the focus of the next session will be: the celebration of the Communion Rite leading to being sent in Mission
- ☐ Invite people to stay for a cup of tea/coffee where applicable
- ☐ Lead or invite another to bring the session to a close with a final prayer.

CLOSING PRAYER
I bind unto myself the name,
The Strong name of the Trinity;
By invocation of the same, The Three in One and One in Three;
Of whom all nature hath creation,
Eternal Father, Spirit, Word;
Praise to the Lord of my Salvation –
Salvation is of Christ the Lord! Amen.

(from St Patrick's Breastplate)

Session Three Handout

Christ is Our Host

At the Last Supper, Christ instituted the Paschal Sacrifice and banquet, by which the Sacrifice of the Cross is continuously made present in the Church. From the days of the apostles, the Church has celebrated that sacrifice by carrying out what the Lord himself did and handed over to his disciples to be done in his memory.

Like him, it has taken bread and wine, given thanks to God over them, broken the bread, and shared the bread and cup of blessing as the Body and Blood of Christ. (*Celebrating the Mystery of Faith*, National Centre for Liturgy, p. 53.)

The Four Actions of the Liturgy of the Eucharist

- Taking
- Blessing
- Breaking
- Sharing

The Journey of the Liturgy of the Eucharist

- Preparation of the Gifts – *Take*
- The Eucharistic Prayer – *Bless*
- The Communion Rite – *Break and Share*

Preparation of the Gifts

The **purpose** of this rite is to make the altar, the gifts that are placed on it and the congregation ready for the Eucharistic offering that is to follow.

The Order of this Rite

- The Altar is dressed with corporal and Missal
- The collection of money and/or other gifts takes place
- The gifts of bread, wine and charity are presented by the people
- The priest says a blessing over the gifts, inaudibly if there is music. If there is no music he may say the blessing audibly, in which case the people respond 'Blessed be God for ever'

This page may be photocopied

Some Parish Suggestions to focus on for the Eucharistic Prayer

- Explore the variety of Eucharistic Prayers available for use
- Explore singing more often as a community
- Sing the acclamations and the opening dialogue
- Posture of the assembly during this prayer – standing, then moving to kneeling
- Encourage families to pray before meals in the home and make the link between that prayer and the Mass.

Further Reading:

National Centre for Liturgy, *Celebrating the Mystery of Faith* (Dublin: Veritas, 2011)

National Centre for Liturgy, *The New Missal: Explaining the Changes* (Dublin: Veritas, 2011)

International Eucharistic Congress 2012, *The Eucharist: Communion With Christ and With One Another: Theological and Pastoral Reflections in Preparation for the 50th International Eucharistic Congress* (Dublin: Veritas, 2011)

- The gifts, altar, cross, priest and people may be incensed
- The priest washes his hands – a ritual gesture of cleansing
- Invitation to people with response, 'Pray brothers and sisters …' to which the people stand to respond
- Prayer over the offering.

Suggestions for Parish Practice

- Have the collection at this time, with enough collectors for it to be carried out promptly
- Have the gifts of bread and wine and the monetary gifts brought forward to the altar from the people
- Bring forward enough hosts to be consecrated and shared with at least a sizeable proportion of the people who have gathered for this Mass
- Present some hosts that can be broken down to be shared at the *Lamb of God*
- Music – suitable sung or instrumental, or occasionally, *silence*
- Enrich this rite with the use of incense
- Moving to a standing posture in readiness for the Eucharistic Prayer.

At this point we are invited to not only offer these gifts of the earth but also the gift of our very selves. We bring ourselves to the table of the Lord for transformation.

The Eucharistic Prayer

- Eucharistic Prayers I, II, III & IV
- Two Eucharistic Prayers for Reconciliation
- Eucharistic Prayer for Use in Masses for Various Needs (including four different forms)
- Three Eucharistic Prayers for use with Children (not contained in the Missal but available for use).

The Elements of this Prayer

- Opening Dialogue ♪
- Preface
- Acclamation – Holy Holy … ♪
- Invocation of the Holy Spirit
- Institution Narrative and Consecration
- Memorial Acclamation ♪
- Memorial of Paschal Mystery and Offering (Invocation of the Holy Spirit)
- Intercessions
- Concluding Doxology with Amen ♪

Changes in Text to the Institution Narrative and Consecration

1. 'Eat *of it*' – the purpose of this insertion is to reference the fact that we, though many, share in the one bread. Therefore we eat *of this* one bread, rather than implying an individual consuming of it in its entirety.
2. The word 'chalice' replaces the word 'cup'. This word, found in the Latin text, was already in the Irish-language version. It is suggestive of a sacred vessel from which more than one person can drink.
3. 'Eternal' replaces the word 'everlasting'. 'Eternal' is found in the Latin text and is a word outside the measure of time, whereas 'everlasting' suggests lasting long in time.
4. 'Poured out' replaces 'shed'. This is to allow for the ambiguity of the text. Only blood is shed, whilst both blood and wine can be poured.
5. The new translation also replaces the phrase 'for all' with the phrase 'for many'. This translates what is found in the Latin text, *pro multis*, and is also what is found in the accounts of the Last Supper in Mark and in Paul's Letter to the Corinthians. This is not intended to imply that God's love is limited or that Christ did not die on the cross for all men and women. Rather it acknowledges that human beings may choose whether or not to accept the gift of salvation. The Church's enduring teaching, however, continues to be that Christ's salvation is for all.

Session Four

We are Sent to Become What We Have Received

Structured Overview

Purpose of the Session

To explore the enactment of the Communion Rite and the Concluding Rites of the Mass, highlighting the gift we receive in the Body of Christ and the missionary imperative of Eucharist – becoming what we receive in and for the world. The session begins with a focus on the human experience of being committed to a particular action and what that entails. The session, in turn, draws on the experience of Emmaus and the natural response of action that the two demonstrated. Appropriately, through an exploration of the Communion Rite we move to a sense of mission in the Concluding Rites of the Mass, conscious of the source of our nourishment and our ability to live the Eucharist in tangible ways in our lives.

Session Outline*

Welcome & Introductions
Opening Prayer . . . . (10 min)

Movement 1:
Paying attention to our own experience of being motivated to act. . . . . (5 min)

Movement 2:
Hearing the story and reflecting on Emmaus . . . . (5 min)

Movement 3:
Applying the story to our own experience on a Sunday as a community . . . (10 min)

Movement 4:
Exploring the liturgical action of the Communion Rite
and the Dismissal Rite on a Sunday . . . . (20 & 15 min)

Movement 5:
Making concrete suggestions for our own local experience . . . . (10 min)

Closing Prayer

Cuppa

(1 hr 15 min)

The time indicators are, once more, given as guides. From them, leaders can determine the time allocations they will give to each of the movements locally. Leaders might choose to run the session to 1 hr and 30 min.

Checklist immediately prior to a session
- ☐ Set up the room in a warm and inviting manner, with chairs in a semi-circle rather than lecture style.
- ☐ Prepare a prayer focus in the room, for example a covered table with a candle, icon/cross, Bible. Again bread, grapes, wheat can be used.
- ☐ Have any technology needed ready for use before people arrive.
- ☐ Have any handouts/flip chart stand, paper and pens ready for use.
- ☐ Delegate any readings or other tasks to be done before the session begins.
- ☐ Welcome people as they arrive.

When the session begins
- ☐ Welcome people formally to the session. Welcome newcomers in particular to the programme.
- ☐ Introduce yourself and your role in the session.
- ☐ Introduce the session in the context of the programme 'Signposts on the Road to Emmaus' and the purpose of this fourth session.
- ☐ Remind people very briefly of the areas covered to date, namely the Introductory Rites of the Mass, the Liturgy of the Word and the Liturgy of the Eucharist as far as the Doxology and Amen.
- ☐ Let people know the end time and whether or not a cup of tea/coffee is being offered at the end.
- ☐ Give people an opportunity to greet one another.
- ☐ Introduce the Opening Prayer – this can include the lighting of a candle.

Opening Prayer

Invitation to Prayer

Focus

Christ has no body now but yours,
no hands but yours,
no feet but yours.
Yours are the eyes through which
Christ's compassion must look out on the world.
Yours are the feet with which
He is to go about doing good.
Yours are the hands with which
He is to bless us now.

(Attributed to St Teresa of Avila)

Scripture

The cup of blessing that we bless, is it not a sharing in the blood of Christ? The bread that we break, is it not a sharing in the body of Christ? Because there is one bread, we who are many are one body, for we all partake of the one bread.
(1 Corinthians 10:16-17)

To be your bread now, be your wine now,
Lord, come and change us
to be a sign of your love.
Blest and broken, poured and flowing,
gift that you gave us,
to be your body once again.*

Quiet Moment

We take a moment to reflect on how we are signs of God's love in the world.

Prayer

Loving Father, may we always call on you with hearts full of reverence and gratitude.
R. Hallowed be thy name
You feed us with the bread that we need for today, to nourish us for our life's walk on the right path.
R. Give us this day our daily bread.
In times of temptation, trials and testing, we turn to you, God of justice and mercy.
R. Forgive us our trespasses.
We seek to embody your mercy in the face of the hurts and wounds of others, whether friend, family, stranger.
R. Forgive those who trespass against us.

---

* Lyrics from 'To Be Your Bread', by David Haas, GIA Publications Inc., Chicago.

This page may be photocopied

You are greater than any forces that seek to hurt and control us and to lead us down life-denying ways.
R. Deliver us Lord from every evil.

Prayer

Our Father who art in heaven ...

Sign of Peace

Christ has no body but ours. Before we move deeper into this session, we use our bodies as instruments of God as we turn and share with one another a sign of the peace of Christ.

This page may be photocopied

Session Four: We are Sent to Become What We Have Received

Movement 1 (5 min)
Paying attention to our experience of being motivated to act

The aim of this brief exercise is to draw out the key elements of those times in our lives when we felt particularly energised and strongly committed to a specific action or a decision to 'be' in a particular way. The making of a New Year's resolution is one example: what is the motivation behind them? What makes us carry through with them?

Other examples might include being involved in a specific action. If we take the example of a run for charity, we can see a number of things at work. There is:
- A specific cause with which people typically have a personal connection
- The desire to do some good
- A means or way of doing some good
- A recognition of our own ability, of what we can do
- A supportive and encouraging environment
- A shared activity with the sense of belonging and wider involvement that that brings with it.

The point is that when we feel committed to something and invested in it at a personal, individual level and when we feel that we have something to offer, we are more likely to carry it through. At Mass we are individually and collectively commissioned to be in the world in a particular way. The challenge is to help us hear that individual calling in the celebration of the Mass and begin to recognise where that leads us to in our lives.

Leader suggestion: Chart the findings for referencing during the session.

GROUP CONVERSATION
» Can you remember a time in the past when you felt strongly motivated to become part of an action (i.e. a charity event, New Year's resolution or a family project)?
» Where did the motivation come from?
» How did you know you were up to it?

Drawing the feedback together
The leader reminds participants of the key points they have collectively made.

Movement 2 (5 min)
Hearing the story and reflecting on Emmaus

Leader suggestion: Before the session begins, have someone ready to read this Gospel passage, using a Bible.

In these sessions we have been hearing from the story of the two disciples on the road to Emmaus. We heard how they met Jesus along the road as they were leaving Jerusalem and heading for Emmaus. We remember how Jesus broke open their experience for them, beginning with Moses and the Prophets. He then went from being invited to share a meal with them to being the very host of that meal. In the breaking of bread, the two recognised who was in their midst. Tonight we take up that story at this point again and hear the remainder of the story.

READING

A reading from the Holy Gospel according to St Luke (24:30-35)

When he was at the table with them, he took bread, blessed and broke it, and gave it to them. Then their eyes were opened, and they recognised him; and he vanished from their sight. They said to each other, 'Were not our hearts burning within us while he was talking to us on the road, while he was opening the scriptures to us?' That same hour they got up and returned to Jerusalem; and they found the eleven and their companions gathered together. They were saying, 'The Lord has risen indeed, and he has appeared to Simon!' Then they told what had happened on the road, and how he had been made known to them in the breaking of the bread.

The Gospel of the Lord.

REFLECTION
This reflection can be done conversationally with the group. Leaders are invited to make the material their own.

And so we come to the end of the story. And it ends with an action of response on behalf of the two. The first initiative has been with God; remember it was Jesus who broke into their conversation along the road. But the response belongs to the individual.

In this story the two arise from the meal table and return to Jerusalem. There is a sense of resurrection, of a new beginning about their action – they get up. They arise from their despair and they return to Jerusalem. They head out once more on the road but this time when they return to Jerusalem they are nourished by Christ's presence. They go back with the memory of their burning hearts – the passion at their centre that prompts and calls them to action. They now have the faith to understand the events that have happened. So they go back with a new energy and purpose – they go back, carrying their experience with them and seeking out others with whom to share it. In that way they go back with a sense of mission and commission from the Risen Lord.

Movement 3 (10 min)
Applying the story to our own experience on a Sunday as a community

The following notes are given to assist participants to make the link between the experience of the two disciples and their own experience on a Sunday.

Session Four: We are Sent to Become What We Have Received

REFLECTION

When we look to our Sunday experience, there is a real sense of resurrection for us also. In light of what we celebrate and profess in the Mass, we are called to get up – like these two on the road to Emmaus. We are called to arise out of our graves, out of our ways that are not life-giving or nourishing or sustaining. Through our active participation in the celebration of the Mass, our understanding of life and its meaning is shaped and changed. We carry the message of resurrection with us. Jesus died and rose again for us; in baptism we have the promise of this new life.

In light of this new life, we are continually being called and being sent. We have heard the good news and we have been fed by Christ in the Eucharist. Christ has given his very self to us. We are now strengthened and nourished; we are fit for our purpose. Therefore our impulse is to go and do this, go and be this, go and share this. The impulse is to move beyond the confines of the church building and reach out. In every Mass there is an exodus, a time of going out, and we go as people sent, sent to love and serve the Lord in the very ordinary stuff of our lives.

Reflection Questions for the Group
» Within the action of the Mass, where and/or how do we hear messages, calls or invitations to go and live our lives in particular ways?
(Answers might include in the readings, the texts of the prayers, the homily, the dismissal…)
» How and where do we see faith communities putting the call of the Mass into tangible action?

> **Leader suggestion:** Depending on time, discuss the above questions as one group, or have people share with a couple of neighbours and then hear back from people.

Movement 4 (35 min)
Exploring the liturgical action of the Communion Rite and the Dismissal Rite on a Sunday

The following input has two foci: Part 1) the Communion Rite (20 min); and Part 2) the Concluding Rites (15 min).

Leaders are invited to explore with participants these parts of the Mass in turn and the meaning behind them. The following detailed notes for the two parts include reference to changes to texts as found in the new Missal.

PART 1: THE COMMUNION RITE

A reminder from the last time
The four actions of the Liturgy of the Eucharist:
- taking
- blessing
- breaking
- sharing.

Communion Rite: Breaking and Sharing

Within the Communion Rite, we take part in the two Eucharistic actions of breaking and sharing, following the example of Christ in the Last Supper. At the centre of this rite is Christ's present and eternal gift of himself to his Church in the Eucharist.

Journey of the Communion Rite

Map out with people in broad strokes the journey of the Communion Rite and then talk through the Rite using the notes given below.

- Our Father ♪*
- The Rite of Peace
- The Breaking of Bread – Fraction Rite (Lamb of God) ♪*
- Invitation to Communion*
- Communion with procession of the people ♪*
- Silent prayer
- Prayer after Communion

> **Leader suggestion:** Depending on time, the above mapping can be done as a brainstorm with the group.

Leader Background Material and Notes

*In talking through the rite, priority should be given to those parts above marked with an *. These notes are intended as supporting material for the leader and should be used as appropriate for the group.*

Our Father

The Our Father is the great prayer of the baptised. Because of its core themes of daily bread and mutual forgiveness, the Lord's Prayer has been used in all liturgical traditions as a most appropriate preparation for Communion.

♪ This prayer is a gift to us all. While it can be sung, it should only be sung when it is possible for the entire congregation to do so.

The Our Father is expanded by the priest in a prayer that seeks our peace and freedom from sin as we wait for the coming of Christ. The people respond with a doxology that forms the conclusion to the Our Father in many ancient traditions ... *for the kingdom, the power and the glory are yours, now and for ever.*

The Rite of Peace

Before we share in the one Eucharist, the faithful implore peace and unity for the Church and for the whole human family.

This is a preparatory rite and should be perceived as such. It prepares us to do what the focus of the Communion Rite is, namely to receive the Body of Christ. In that way, in its simplicity, it does not overshadow that central action. But it is a powerful reminder to us of the call to be at peace with one another as we receive the Sacrament of Unity.

As a sign, we must mean what we say and do when we exchange peace with another human being – *as such this is another point in the liturgy when we are invited to go and live what we do in our worship.*

The Breaking of Bread – Fraction Rite

This gesture by Christ at the Last Supper gave the entire Eucharistic action its name in the early Church. It takes place during the singing or recitation of the *Agnus Dei*/ 'Lamb of God'.

This breaking of bread is a powerful symbol of the oneness of the congregation as they share in the Eucharist together. Just as many grains of wheat are ground, kneaded and baked together to become one loaf, which is then broken and shared out among many to bring them into one table-fellowship, so those gathered are made one body in the one bread of life which is Christ.

> The bread that we break, is it not the partaking of the Body of the Lord? Because the bread is one, we though many are one body, all of us who partake of the one bread. (*1 Cor 10:16-17*)

In this action there is a wonderful sense of nature's process of breaking down and building up. Even the term 'Fraction Rite' tells us something. Remember your school fractions: the breaking down of a whole into parts which are always held in relationship to the whole, i.e. a half of ... a third of ... a quarter of ...

On any given Sunday, a congregation/assembly is one but made up of many parts. Like the Eucharist, we too are broken. People's lives may carry the hurt of brokenness. Through Eucharist, the people of God are called to fullness of life, to unity, to completeness. This fraction rite echoes the reality of the broken Body of Christ on a journey to wholeness in Christ.

For all the above reasons then, hopefully, in our parishes we get to see and witness at least some of the hosts that are consecrated during the liturgy being broken down at this stage of the liturgy, in order to be shared with some of the faithful during Communion. In practice, this means sourcing the larger hosts that are available for use.

♪ If a musical setting is used, it can continue until the action of breaking the consecrated hosts is complete by using additional phrases that are available in many of the settings, always finishing with 'Lamb of God ... grant us peace ...'

Invitation to Communion

In the invitation to Communion we find changes in the wording to more accurately translate what is in the Latin text of the Missal. In these changes we also see a closer alignment to the original scriptural reference.

'Behold the Lamb of God, behold him who takes away the sins of the world.' Recall the words of John the Baptist as Jesus approaches the waters of the Jordan for baptism. (*John 1:29*)

'Blessed are those called to the supper of the Lamb'. The angel's words to John in the Book of Revelation. (Revelation 19:9)

Again in the change from 'Happy' to 'Blessed', there is a recognition that there is a difference between being happy and being blessed. We can probably all look back on our lives and see moments when, although we may have been far from happy, we were very much blessed.

The people's response to this invitation has also undergone some changes. 'Lord I am not worthy that you should enter under my roof but only say the word and my soul shall be healed.' The scriptural reference here is to Matthew 8:8 and the words of the Roman centurion seeking the healing of his servant. The centurion stands as a model of faith for us as we approach Communion. Do we come with similar faith and belief in the gift and healing power of the Eucharist? Again the nourishment and healing of Eucharist is not confined to the physical but also focuses on the very core of our being and who we are.

Communion Procession with Communion

This is one of the most important actions of the assembly/congregation. As a Church, we are a pilgrim people and pilgrims walk, together. The Communion procession is a symbol of the unity of the people who have gathered to celebrate this Eucharist as the Body of Christ. In this moment we receive back our humble gifts of bread and wine as the richest gift of God's love – the Body and Blood of Christ.

♪ We are supported in our common journey together through the use of an appropriate communion hymn, which speaks of and serves the action that we are undertaking in this moment of the liturgy. Hopefully, music ministers lead us in chants or hymns with which the journeying assembly can join in singing at least a simple refrain.

> Faith demands that we approach the Eucharist fully aware that we are approaching Christ himself. The Eucharist is a mystery of presence, the perfect fulfilment of Jesus' promise to remain with us until the end of the world.
>
> (Pope John Paul II, *Mane Nobiscum Domine*, 16)

This quote reminds us that the action of processing and receiving Communion is one that calls for reverence and hospitality. We welcome Christ, really and substantially present, once more into our lives. We are called to reverence and hospitality towards what we are receiving and towards those with whom we make this journey to Communion, the Body of Christ.

Take and Eat, Take and Drink

At the heart of the Eucharistic Prayer, we heard once more Christ's command to us to 'Take and eat ... take and drink'. In light of this command then, it is most desirable that the faithful share from the chalice.

'Drinking at the Eucharist is:
- a sharing in the sign of the new covenant (cf. Luke 22:20)
- a foretaste of the heavenly banquet (cf. Matthew 26:29)
- a sign of the participation in the suffering Christ (cf. Mark 10:38-39).'

(*Celebrating the Mystery of Faith*, p. 56)

In the context of Ireland, the Irish Episcopal Conference sought and received permission from Rome in 1991 for 'Holy Communion to be distributed under both kinds to the faithful at Masses on Sundays and holydays of obligation and on weekdays, if, in the judgement of the ordinary (Bishop) Communion can be given in an orderly and reverent way.' (*Liturgical Calendar for Ireland 2012*, Veritas)

Hosts Consecrated at this Mass

The *General Instruction of the Roman Missal* highlights the offering of the chalice in paragraph 85 as well as highlighting the desirability of receiving hosts consecrated at the same Mass. This underscores that our Communion is a participation in the sacrifice actually being celebrated.

Coming to Communion is the highpoint and culmination of the Eucharistic celebration. In this moment of Communion we get to welcome Christ into our lives – to receive Christ and to become what we have received. Saint Augustine said: 'Behold what you are, become what you receive.' Our Amen to 'The Body of Christ' is an 'Amen' to the truth that:
- The Consecrated Host is the Body of Christ
- I am the Body of Christ
- We as a gathered community are the Body of Christ.

(The Triple Amen of Augustine)

Communion to those unable to be present

Becoming what we receive is an ongoing and real invitation to live Eucharist in our lives. When at this point in our liturgy we send ministers of Holy Communion to bring communion to the sick, we are once more giving ourselves a reminder of the call to reach out in a tangible way from the celebration of the Mass, from the Eucharist.

Silence

In a time of prayerful silence we are given an opportunity to give thanks for what we have received, to offer our personal prayer to God and to ready ourselves to go out and live what we have celebrated. The rubrics indicate that we can choose individually whether to sit or kneel for this time of personal prayer.

Prayer after Communion

Before we are sent out, the presiding priest leads us in the Prayer after Communion. We pray that what we have celebrated and received will now bear fruit in our lives. As in other prayers in the liturgy which are led by the priest and to which we give our assent in an Amen, priest and people **stand** together for this prayer and continue to stand to the end of Mass.

Parish suggestions for Communion Rite
- Communion under both kinds on occasion
- Fraction Rite – breaking down of some hosts
- Greater sharing of hosts that have been consecrated at the Mass
- Look to communion procession – hospitality and reverence
- Communion to the sick and those not able to be present
- Ongoing training and formation for Extraordinary Ministers of Holy Communion as well as regular housekeeping
- Music ministers – looking to music that accompanies the procession and a sung setting of the 'Lamb of God'.

Part 2: Journey of the Concluding Rite

Purpose
The Mass closes with a brief Concluding Rite. Its purpose is to send the people forth to put into effect in their daily lives the Paschal Mystery and the Unity in Christ, which they have celebrated. They are given a sense of abiding mission. This mission calls them to witness to Christ in the world and to bring the Gospel to the poor. (*Celebrating the Mystery of Faith*, p. 62)

Once more the leader maps out the journey of the Concluding Rites with the group and in turn unpacks the journey.

- Brief Announcements
- Greeting and blessing
- Dismissal
- People's response
- Recessional Procession ♪

The Concluding Rite is intended to be brief, and necessarily so, because having celebrated Eucharist we now need to get out there and live it. We need to be sent.

Brief Announcements
These *brief* notices may help the people to make the transition from worship into renewed Christian witness in society; the place where we live the liturgy after the liturgy!

Greeting and Blessing
Again we find the change in wording here as in other instances in the liturgy: 'The Lord be with you – And with your spirit.' This greeting helps people to focus on the blessing that is to follow. This blessing can be either solemn or a simple prayer over the people. In the new edition of the Missal, for each of the days of Lent we find new prayers that can be used. All conclude with the Trinitarian formula during which the assembly mark themselves with the Sign of the Cross.

Dismissal and Response
There are now four alternative dismissals provided. These are all based on the Latin *Ite, missa est*. This phrase can be translated as a clear dismissal of the people from Mass or as an announcement that the Mass has ended. It can also carry a missionary call. In *Sacramentum Caritatis*, Pope Benedict XVI wrote: 'These few words succinctly express the missionary nature of the Church. The People of God might be helped to understand more clearly this essential dimension of the Church's life, taking the dismissal as a starting-point.' The dismissals are as follows:
- Go forth, the Mass is ended
- Go and announce the Gospel of the Lord
- Go in peace, glorifying the Lord by your life
- Go in peace.

To which the people respond: 'Thanks be to God'. This is a statement of grateful praise for encountering the risen Christ in our worship. The hope is that the people are sent forth, just as the two on the road to Emmaus, with a sense of mission and commission from the Risen Lord to live what we have experienced.

Recessional Procession

This procession of priest and ministers functions to lead the assembly out of the worship space. No music is prescribed for this procession, though typically we experience either instrumental or a sung hymn at this point. A hymn that speaks of mission and Christian action can help strengthen the sense of going and living what we have celebrated. However, music ministers need not take offence if people leave during this hymn, given that they have already been dismissed!

Two quotes to help us unpack the meaning behind this Rite

The following two quotes are helpful in bringing us deeper into the meaning and intent of the Concluding Rites.

> *Leader suggestion:* Read these quotes out, or ask someone else to, and look for people's response to them.

'The Eucharist compels all who believe in him to become "bread that is broken" for others, and to work for the building of a more just and fraternal world. Keeping in mind the multiplication of the loaves and fishes, we need to realise that Christ continues today to exhort his disciples to become personally engaged: "You yourselves, give them something to eat" (Mt 14:16). Each of us is truly called, together with Jesus, to be bread broken for the life of the world.'

(Pope Benedict XVI, Sacramentum Caritatis, 88)

'In each of our lives Jesus comes as the Bread of Life – to be eaten, to be consumed by us. This is how he loves us. Then Jesus comes in our human life as the hungry one, the other, hoping to be fed with the Bread of our life, our hearts by loving, and our hands by serving. In loving and serving, we prove that we have been created in the likeness of God, for God is Love and when we love we are like God.'

(Blessed Teresa of Calcutta)

Reflection Question for Group

'Go and announce the Gospel of the Lord' – how might we do this?

Viewed from this lens, then, Sunday Mass is not about getting our weekly duty over and done with but rather is about linking what we celebrate on a Sunday with how we live the rest of the week. Liturgy is not a consciousness-raising exercise. Liturgy is our worship of God. 'But in worshipping God, we are challenged in a way that no other exercise would challenge us: we are called to be what we celebrate.' (*Celebrating the Mystery of Faith*, p. 79)

> ## Parish suggestions for Concluding Rite
> - Brief notices
> - Use of newsletter to promote opportunities for outreach
> - Posture – standing at Prayer after Communion to the end of Mass.

Movement 5 (10 min or to end)
Making concrete suggestions for our own local experience

> **Leader suggestion:** Make sure to record in some way what people say and to have a local forum to which the feedback can be brought.

» In light of our exploration tonight, are there one or two things you would like to affirm in what you are doing as a parish?
» Are there one or two things you might suggest that you would like to see tried in the parish in the coming months?

If time allows, have participants chat about the above for a few minutes with a neighbour and then hear from the wider group. Otherwise process the questions with the group immediately. Let people know that you will pass on what has been recommended to the local parish for the awareness of those who prepare the liturgy.

WRAP-UP & CLOSING PRAYER

LEADER NOTE: CHECKLIST FOR CLOSE OF SESSION
- ☐ Remind people of what they have explored in the session.
- ☐ This is the last of four independent sessions. Thank people for giving of their time and themselves in any of the sessions they attended.
- ☐ Encourage them to take what they have explored with them in their hearts, that it may lead to action – like the two on the road to Emmaus.
- ☐ Take the opportunity to make any other announcements of relevance to the local situation and/or to invite people to ways of actively applying what they have explored.
- ☐ Invite people to stay for a cup of tea/coffee where applicable.
- ☐ Lead or invite another to bring the session to a close with a final prayer.

CLOSING PRAYER

REFLECTION

'The Church at this moment may be likened to the disciples on the road to Emmaus. Like them, we continue to speak with one another about all that God has been doing in our midst. Like them, we are on the road, in via, amidst a journey, and, like them, many of our expectations have been unsettled. As our tightly held expectations are disturbed, the gift of the Lord's presence, the power of the Holy Spirit, is ours to receive, and the Lord is in our midst, no less than on the road to Emmaus – as companion on the journey, as teacher, as guide and, especially, in the Blessing and Breaking of the Eucharistic Bread.'
(Cardinal Mahoney and the Priests of the Archdiocese of Los Angeles, *As I have done for you: A Pastoral Letter on Ministry*, 2000)

TOGETHER WE PRAY

Rush upon us O Spirit of God!
From this time on, rush upon us, like living water,
like leaping fire, like fresh breath through an open window.
For this time, rush upon us, O Holy Spirit, with
wisdom and knowledge, with understanding and counsel,
with wonder and recognition and awe.
Just in time, rush upon us O Spirit of God,
in life-giving words, in songs from the voiceless,
in a passion for witness.
At this time, rush upon us, O Holy Spirit,
this hopeful time, this searching time, this preparing time,
this coming and going time, this trusting time,
this new time, this full time.
ALL THE TIME, rush upon us, O Spirit of God!*

---

* Holy Spirit Prayer: available at ppc.catholic.org.au.

Further Reading:

National Centre for Liturgy, *Celebrating the Mystery of Faith* (Dublin: Veritas, 2011)

National Centre for Liturgy, *The New Missal: Explaining the Changes* (Dublin: Veritas, 2011)

International Eucharistic Congress 2012, *The Eucharist: Communion With Christ and With One Another: Theological and Pastoral Reflections in Preparation for the 50th International Eucharistic Congress* (Dublin: Veritas, 2011)

Session Four Handout

We are Sent to Become what We have Received

The Journey of the Communion Rite

- Our Father ♪
- The Rite of Peace
- The Breaking of Bread – Fraction Rite (Lamb of God) ♪
- Invitation to Communion
- Communion with procession of the people ♪
- Silent prayer
- Prayer after Communion

Our Father: *The great prayer of the baptised with themes of daily bread and mutual forgiveness.*

The Rite of Peace: *A tangible reminder to us of the call to be at peace with one another as we receive the sacrament of unity.*

The Breaking of Bread – Fraction Rite (Lamb of God): *A powerful symbol of the oneness of the congregation as they share in the Eucharist together.*

Invitation to Communion: *Behold the Lamb of God who takes away the sins of the world* (cf. John 1:29).
Blessed are those called to the supper of the Lamb (cf. Revelation 19:9).
Lord I am not worthy … (cf. Matthew 8:8).

Communion Procession with Communion: *A symbol of the unity of the congregation as they receive the Body and Blood of Christ.* Paragraph 85 of the Roman Missal highlights:

1. The importance of receiving hosts consecrated at the same Mass
2. The value of following the command of Christ to 'Take and drink …' as
   - a sign of the new covenant (Luke 22:20);
   - a foretaste of the heavenly banquet (Matthew 26:29);
   - a sign of our participation in the suffering of Christ (cf. Mark 10:38-39).

'Behold what you are, become what you receive.' (St Augustine)

This page may be photocopied

Silence: *We give thanks for what we have received and ready ourselves to go out and live what we have celebrated. We can choose to sit or kneel for this personal prayer to God.*

Prayer after Communion: *We stand and pray that what we have celebrated will bear fruit in our lives.*

Parish Suggestions for Communion Rite

- Communion under both kinds on occasion
- Fraction Rite – breaking down of some hosts
- Greater sharing of hosts that have been consecrated at Mass
- Look to communion procession – hospitality and reverence
- Communion to the sick and those not able to be present
- Ongoing training and formation for Extraordinary Ministers of Holy Communion as well as regular housekeeping
- Music ministers – looking to music that accompanies the procession and a sung setting of the 'Lamb of God'.

The Purpose and Journey of the Concluding Rite

The Mass closes with a brief Concluding Rite. Its purpose is to send the people forth to put into effect in their daily lives the Paschal Mystery and the Unity in Christ, which they have celebrated. They are given a sense of abiding mission. This mission calls them to witness to Christ in the world and to bring the Gospel to the poor. (*Celebrating the Mystery of Faith*, p. 62)

- Brief Announcements
- Greeting and blessing
- Dismissal
- People's response
- Recessional Procession ♪

New Dismissals from the Mass

- Go forth, the Mass is ended
- Go and announce the Gospel of the Lord
- Go in peace, glorifying the Lord by your life
- Go in peace.

Parish Suggestions for the Concluding Rite

- Brief notices
- Use of newsletter to promote opportunities for outreach
- Posture – standing at the Prayer after Communion to the end of Mass.

'The Eucharist compels all who believe in him to become "bread that is broken" for others, and to work for the building of a more just and fraternal world. Keeping in mind the multiplication of the loaves and fishes, we need to realise that Christ continues today to exhort his disciples to become personally engaged: "You, yourselves, give them something to eat" (Mt 14:16). Each of us is truly called, together with Jesus, to be bread broken for the life of the world.'

(*Pope Benedict XVI, Sacramentum Caritatis, 88*)

'In each of our lives Jesus comes as the Bread of Life – to be eaten, to be consumed by us. This is how he loves us. Then Jesus comes in our human life as the hungry one, the other, hoping to be fed with the Bread of our life, our hearts by loving, and our hands by serving. In loving and serving, we prove that we have been created in the likeness of God, for God is Love and when we love we are like God.'

(*Blessed Teresa of Calcutta*)

A Reflective Session

Preparation and Outline

Content

This 1 hour and 30 minute reflection session uses the Gospel story of the two disciples on the road to Emmaus as its backdrop. As this story unfolds, links are made with our own understanding and experience of Eucharist, our own participation in the Eucharist and the life we are called to in the Eucharistic celebration.

Participants

This session was originally intended for liturgical ministers. However, as presented, it can be used with a broad section of people in a variety of settings. Any members of a worship community in a parish, educational institution or other setting can beneficially engage with this material.

How to use this material

Below is a template and proposed content for the session. Adaptations can readily be made to accommodate the circumstances of the session and the people engaging in it. Those leading the session might decide to use different music or different visuals. They might also decide to add to or take away from the given input and reflection questions. The key thing is to make the adjustments that are right for the group that will be engaging in it.

PowerPoint Slides

PowerPoint slides have been prepared for this session and can be downloaded from the following link: veritasbooksonline.com/signpostsontheroadtoemmaus/resources

Possible Needs

1 facilitator
1 prayer leader
1 reader (3/6 people to enact reading – optional)
1 person to share/deliver reflections after each section of reading
1 song leader
A CD player and music
A Bible from which to proclaim the readings
A prayer focus: a table with bread, grapes and wine cup, icon/cross …

Room Set-up

- Have the seating arranged in a semi-circle arrangement with a central aisle down the middle. Let this central aisle be your 'road image' so that it may be curved from the back to the front of the room

- At the end of this 'road', have a table set with bread, grapes and wine cup
- Set up a PowerPoint/overhead projector against the front wall where people can see it
- Depending on the time of day, think about how the lighting and heating will be in the room and let this work to your best advantage
- Decide if you need any amplification or if people will be able to hear what is happening.

Session Pattern

The following outlines the path of the session. Again, this is given as a template that can be adapted to meet local needs and circumstances.

- Welcome
- Opening prayer

> Reading
> Reflection
> Silence – with reflection question
> Brief Sharing
> Sung Response: Hymn Verse
> (This pattern is repeated four times)

- Closing Reflection and Prayer
- Hospitality – cuppa!

Session Material

WELCOME (*Facilitator*)
Before people gather, try to make the venue as warm and inviting as possible. Have everything in place so that you are not hurrying around getting ready as people arrive but are available to greet and welcome people informally.

Instrumental music can be playing in the room to help create the atmosphere for the session.

When people have gathered, welcome them to this session. Let them know that this is an opportunity to think about the Mass perhaps from a different perspective than we normally do. This is a time for reflection and making connections with the word of God and their own experience.

Give them an indication of how long their time together will be and if there will be a cup of tea at the end.

OPENING PRAYER (*Facilitator or prayer leader*)
'As we begin this time we do so in a spirit of prayer and reflection and so we begin by **standing** and marking ourselves with the sign of our baptism (The sign of the Cross)'.

A REFLECTIVE SESSION

Loving God,
you call us together in this time, in this place.
Let us know your presence among us
as we share this journey of exploration and prayer.
We ask this in the name of your Son, our Lord Jesus Christ. Amen.
People are invited to be seated to listen to the Word of God.

READING I

The reader proclaims the Gospel from the front of the room, perhaps beside an icon of Christ. While the reading is taking place, two people come from the back of the room and follow the path made through the people – in conjunction with what is being read so that a third person joins them on the road in this first passage. These three hold their pose at the end of this passage for a few moments and then sit on the floor while the reflection is taking place.

A reading from the Holy Gospel according to St Luke (24:13-18)

Now on that same day two of them were going to a village called Emmaus, about seven miles from Jerusalem, and talking with each other about all these things that had happened.
While they were talking and discussing, Jesus himself came near and went with them, but their eyes were kept from recognising him.
And he said to them, 'What are you discussing with each other while you walk along?' They stood still, looking sad. Then one of them, whose name was Cleopas, answered him, 'Are you the only stranger in Jerusalem who does not know the things that have taken place there in these days?'
He asked them, 'What things?' They replied, 'The things about Jesus of Nazareth ...'

The Gospel of the Lord.

REFLECTION I *(Facilitator or another)*

This is the beginning of a story with which we are very familiar – the Emmaus story. But perhaps for the next while we might sit with this opening part of the story and tease out what it can speak to us of 'gathering'.

'Now on that same day two of them were going to a village ...' We enter into the story of these two, in the middle of a journey, from Jerusalem to a place about seven miles away, Emmaus. *Who were these two on the road?* We are not really told much about them. We are given the name Cleopas, the one and only time he is mentioned in the Gospel accounts. But we are not told anything about his companion: was it a man or a woman; perhaps they were a married couple; perhaps they were two men. We just don't know.

What are they doing? They are talking about what had been happening and the events in Jerusalem. They are full of the news of the day.
How are they feeling as they discuss the news of the day? Remember, these two had gone in hope to Jerusalem. Now they were now returning to Emmaus filled with disappointment and sadness, no doubt confused and with heavy hearts.

Today, in our meetings with others, what might the news be? What are we hearing in the news these days: perhaps natural disasters, bailouts, job losses, drugs, political upheaval and fallouts, world, national and local events of importance and interest to us.

> ***Leader suggestion:*** Headlines from the week's papers might be read out to participants.

We talk about the events of our days and in doing so we are really trying to figure out how this impacts us, who we are in all of this – individually and collectively.
We return to our story of the two on the road. A stranger comes along the road and breaks into their journey. This stranger engages with them, he wants to become part of their conversation, he risks taking the initiative to enter into relationship with them.

He asks them a question: 'What are you discussing …?' They could reject him, turn away from him, or tell him firmly to mind his own business. But they don't. They allow him in. They welcome him into their midst. We, with the benefit of hindsight, know what gift they give to themselves as a result of their action of hospitality, and this hospitality is the hallmark of Christian gathering. It is the first action, the first impulse, the first movement of every Christian gathering – the movement outward towards another, a movement of welcome, inclusion, reverence. This is a key understanding to carry with us as we come together to worship our God.

Now let's stop and let's imagine our Sunday experience. As we make our way to church on a Sunday or Saturday evening, we are all coming from different places with some common experiences and some unique ones. We make the journey to our churches from all different starting points, carrying different life experiences and emotions. Our minds can be full of the happenings and encounters of the week – global, local and personal – but we move in a common direction.

And at some point in our journey towards Mass we begin to meet one another – getting out of the car, moving through the door of the church, as we bless ourselves with holy water, as we take our seat in the pew. We find ourselves alongside others, young and old, friend, neighbour, acquaintance and stranger. How is that meeting? How do we see that stranger? Do we acknowledge them? Is it part of our consciousness even to say hello, to greet them?

In the story, the two did not know it was Christ. We are told that their eyes were kept from recognising Jesus; something within them prevented them from recognising the risen Lord. Yet they welcomed him into their story. They welcomed this stranger in their midst. This is a key point in Luke's story: welcoming the stranger is a key to celebrating Eucharist. Just think of the lost opportunity if they had turned their backs. Think of what they would have missed out on if they had told him to keep to himself.

These two, whoever they are, have given us a model of communion and ministry. In being welcoming, in including the stranger in our journey, we are welcoming Christ.
On a Sunday we get to welcome Christ *in the congregation*, in the assembly. We are the Body of Christ.

> 'For where two or three are gathered in my name, I am there among them.' (Matthew 18:20)

A Reflective Session

When we gather to pray, Christ is present. In the midst of that assembly we get to meet the risen Lord week in and week out. From the first moments of the liturgy Christ is present. From these first moments we are called into communion with Christ and with one another.

Our invitation on a Sunday when we gather to celebrate Mass is to reach out and welcome Christ in our midst. This impacts what we do even before Mass begins and what we do during the Introductory Rites of the Mass.

Silence – with reflection question
Facilitator: Imagine yourself in those gathering moments of Mass, imagine yourself walking into the church building and taking your place … now look and recognise Christ around you. And when you have done this you might like to reflect on the question: 'Where and how do I see my faith community as welcoming?'

Sharing
Facilitator: Invite participants to share with their neighbour one thought they had during the quiet time.

Sung response: Verse 2 of 'The Servant Song' by Richard Gillard
Facilitator/Prayer leader invites participants to stand *and join in singing one verse of this or another suitable hymn.*

'We are pilgrims on a journey; we are travellers on the road;
We are here to help each other walk the mile and bear the load.'

Reading II
The reader takes his/her place at the front of the room while the three enacting the scene resume their places. Having continued walking for a few steps, the 'Christ' figure could gesture to the two to sit on the ground while the 'Christ' figure sits on a chair (akin to a reading pose).

> A reading from the Holy Gospel according to Luke (24:19-27)
>
> He asked them, 'What things?' They replied, 'The things about Jesus of Nazareth, who was a prophet mighty in deed and word before God and all the people, and how our chief priests and leaders handed him over to be condemned to death and crucified him. But we had hoped that he was the one to redeem Israel. Yes, and besides all this, it is now the third day since these things took place. Moreover, some women of our group astounded us. They were at the tomb early this morning, and when they did not find his body there, they came back and told us that they had indeed seen a vision of angels who said that he was alive. Some of those who were with us went to the tomb and found it just as the women had said; but they did not see him.'
>
> Then he said to them, 'Oh, how foolish you are, and how slow of heart to believe all that the prophets have declared! Was it not necessary that the Messiah should suffer these things and then enter into his glory?' Then beginning with Moses and all the prophets, he interpreted to them the things about himself in all the scriptures.
>
> The Gospel of the Lord

REFLECTION II (*Facilitator or another*)
Words, words, words, we hear a lot of words in our world. From all angles we seem to be bombarded with words. But we have a new phenomenon of late – the buzzword and more particularly the sound bite. The goal of many communicators these days is to get that sound bite lodged into people's brains. Our response can be to grow tired of words and to grow sceptical of sound bites. We can be wary of the messages people are bringing to us. But oh how foolish and how slow of heart we would be if we closed our selves to the words of scripture.

We think again of those two travellers on the road, journeying from Jerusalem to Emmaus. How do you think that they were feeling? We are told sad, but probably also confused, shocked, perhaps angry. Angry at the authorities, at Jesus, at themselves and their own foolishness. Remember they are getting out of Jerusalem, heading back home. They had put their trust in this new prophet who was mighty in word and deed. But this mighty prophet, this one who was supposed to redeem Israel, ended up crucified like a common criminal. This is not how it was supposed to be.

And what do they go on to tell us? It's three days since his death, time has moved on and there seems to be no hope. They know of the empty tomb but fail to understand its meaning.

If they had really heard and listened to the prophets they would understand, but they haven't. Instead they have lived through the experience and have failed to grasp its meaning. And without this understanding they fail to recognise the risen Lord in their presence.

Yet what does Jesus do? He takes the messengers of God's word, beginning with Moses and the prophets, and he unpacks their message for the travellers. Moreover, he explains to them how it all relates to Jesus. By doing so he is able to help the two travellers begin their journey to making sense of what they have just gone through in Jerusalem.

There are 3 steps here: **proclamation, interpretation, reception**, and we see these steps at play in our Mass every week.

Let's reflect on that first step, the step of **Proclamation**. The word has to be spoken out loud – it then becomes real. We know that in life. We can go about for years with things unspoken – when said they become real, they become something we have to, get to, face and take on board. But we need prophets – people who will speak God's message to us. In our world we still have plenty of prophets. Every day we encounter God's prophets in our lives. We encounter people who knowingly or unknowingly speak a message of God to us. In our liturgy on a Sunday we also have our prophets. Who are they?

They are our Readers – those ministers of the liturgy who speak to us a message from God. They are the ones who say out loud the words of salvation. They utter into being God's words of love and healing. In the midst of the assembly they take their place and proclaim aloud our stories – stories that are not about buzzwords or the latest sound bites. These stories are about the lives of those who believe in and share in the promise of resurrection.

These stories are not about what God did in the past but about what God is doing upon us now. We are told:

> When the sacred scriptures are read in the Church, God himself speaks to his people, and Christ, present in his own words, proclaims the Gospel. (*General Instruction on the Roman Missal*, 29)

In these stories God speaks to us today and calls us into relationship with him, a relationship that brings us life in abundance, not mediocrity.

The reader articulates these stories in faith and through faith so that they can be received into the very being of those who have gathered.

But how do we interpret these words: we need to take the next step, that of **Interpretation**. On any given Sunday, the presence of Christ in the words of Scripture meets the presence of Christ in the very stuff of people's lives. We hear particular stories, particular messages in the context of a particular season in the Church year. If these are not to be mere sound bites, what difference do these words make? How do I receive these words into my life and shape my life as a result of them?

The task of the priest celebrant is to help us to do just that. He takes the proclaimed word and interprets it, hopefully, always in light of the resurrected Christ and in the context of the lives of the assembly who have gathered. His task is to help break open the word of God into the centre of our lives.

But no matter how rich the homily, how good the interpretation, at the end of the day the final step is up to us: **Reception**. This is because the journey from proclaimed word to interpreted word to lived word demands that the final action is ours. God gifts us with this word but ours is the initiative of response or non-response. Every day we make choices, take decisions, turn in particular directions, and act in particular ways.

The first choice that we are invited to make is to be authentic listeners of this proclaimed and interpreted word. And authentic listening can only result in a lived-out response.

But remember, Christ came that we might have life in abundance. Sometimes that life may not be what, where or when we expect it but part of our listening to God is a listening to see God's word in action in our lives. Christ is present in the midst of the faithful through his word. It is our choice to welcome this presence into our lives and to allow God's word to speak to us in the rhythm of our lives.

We do this as individuals but we also do this as a community. This is why we can stand with one another in response to the word and profess our shared belief in the Creed. This is why we can offer our common petitions to God – asking for the needs of the whole world and not just ourselves.

Silence – with reflection question

Facilitator: Imagine yourself in the assembly listening to the proclamation of the Word of God. What one thing would help your hearing of the word of God?

Sharing

Facilitator: Invite participants to share with their neighbour one thought they had during the quiet time.

Sung response: Verse 3 of 'The Servant Song' by Richard Gillard

Facilitator/Prayer leader invites participants to stand and join in singing one verse of this or another suitable hymn.

'I will hold the Christ light for you in the night time of your fear;
I will hold my hand out to you, speak the peace you long to hear.'

Reading III

The reader takes his/her place at the front of the room while the three people enacting the scene resume their places. Having continued walking for a few steps, the two gesture to the 'Christ' figure to join them at the table and they take their places around the table in time to the reading – to the point where the 'Christ' figure leaves.

A reading from the Holy Gospel according to Luke (24:28-32)

As they came near the village to which they were going, he walked ahead as if he were going on. But they urged him strongly, saying, 'Stay with us, because it is almost evening and the day is now nearly over.' So he went in to stay with them. When he was at the table with them, he took bread, blessed and broke it, and gave it to them. Then their eyes were opened, and they recognised him; and he vanished from their sight. They said to each other, 'Were not our hearts burning within us while he was talking to us on the road, while he was opening the scriptures to us?'

The Gospel of the Lord.

Reflection III (*Facilitator or another*)
Once more we see in this Gospel passage an action that is at the heart of our liturgy and our ministry: an action of hospitality and welcome. We have Jesus making as if to leave (though clearly he had no intention of doing so) and the two urge him to stay with them. They urge him not just to stay, but to stay *with* them, stay in this relationship.

We see here a very human impulse at work: the impulse to stay with something good, to prolong the good experience. We see the natural impulse to want to continue in an experience in which we find nourishment. They have been fed by word and now, aware of their hunger for more, they will be fed by bread.

And in this story we see a very simple but significant reversal in roles. Christ moves from being the guest to being the host. The two invite him to dine with them. They provide the setting and the provisions for the meal. But Christ is clearly the host of the meal. And it is Christ who leads the eucharistic actions of taking, blessing, breaking and sharing.

On a Sunday we set the table for the Eucharist, we prepare the space, but in every Eucharist Christ is the host. We as a community get to prepare our worship, to set the scene, but it is Christ who prays in us and who leads our prayer.

Think of the image of meal and bread at the heart of this encounter. There is something deeply intimate about the sharing of food. Food is fraught with images of companionship, community, sharing, feast, giving of self. Food and drink becomes part of who you are – you are what you eat!

Bread itself is the staff of life. It sustains us. It represents our basic, daily nourishment. But it also represents the gift of God's creation and our participation in God's work – 'fruit of the earth and work of human hands'. As the land yields its harvest we give of ourselves and of our labour in the fashioning of bread from the grains of wheat.

For a moment let's turn our attention back to these travelling companions. They quite literally, as companions, broke bread together in their shared meal. In that human interaction we find hospitality, fellowship, nourishment, thanksgiving. In the intimacy of a meal, in the taking, blessing, breaking and sharing of bread, they recognise for the first time who is in their midst – **they recognise Christ. And now they can begin to understand the sacrifice of the Cross.**

So they recognise Christ and what happens? He vanishes. In the moment they recognise him, he is gone. They move from a real presence to a seeming absence in an instant. But that seeming absence, that emptiness now has a totally new meaning and content, for now that emptiness is full of Christ's presence.

So the two disciples don't panic. They don't call out for Christ to come back; they don't despair. Rather they remember and they continue to recognise. They look back and they remember and recognise the burning of their hearts as Christ had unpacked God's word for them; they recognise Christ in the stranger who had walked with them; they recognise now the abiding presence of Christ despite his apparent absence.

Having walked with Christ, having listened to his Word and shared in his meal, these two disciples believe and know that Christ is indeed present – even where there appears to be absence. Now they can truly begin to understand the events of Jerusalem and see them not in despair but in hope and joy.

On a Sunday, ministers of communion engage in sharing the nourishment and presence of Christ with us – they share in being a presence of Christ. When we say 'Amen' to the Body of Christ, we remember the triple Amen of Augustine: yes, I am the Body of Christ, yes, we are the Body of Christ, yes, this is the Body of Christ.

Christ is with us. This is the awesome gift of God. And so perhaps like these two disciples at Emmaus, we can look to our own experiences, our own encounters and begin to see the presence of Christ at work, we can begin to recognise the burning of our hearts that leads us to life-giving ways of Christian joy and hope.

Silence – with reflection question
Facilitator: They recognised him and he vanished from their sight. Where can you look back and see the presence of Christ at work in your life/the world?

Sharing
Facilitator: Invite participants to share with their neighbour one thought they had during the quiet time.

Sung response: Verse 1 of 'The Servant Song' by Richard Gillard
Facilitator/Prayer leader invites participants to stand *and join in singing one verse of this or another suitable hymn.*

'Will you let me be your servant, let me be as Christ to you;
Pray that I may have the grace to let you be my servant too.'

Reading IV
The reader takes his/her place at the front of the room while the two enacting the part of the two disciples resume their places. As the reading is proclaimed, the two retrace their path back to 'Jerusalem' to an awaiting group at the back of the room.

> A reading from the Holy Gospel according to Luke (24:33-35)
>
> That same hour they got up and returned to Jerusalem; and they found the eleven and their companions gathered together. They were saying, 'The Lord has risen indeed, and he has appeared to Simon!' Then they told what had happened on the road, and how he had been made known to them in the breaking of the bread.
>
> The Gospel of the Lord.

Reflection IV
And so we come to the end of the story. And it ends with an action of response on behalf of the two. The first initiative has been with God, remember it was Jesus who broke into their conversation along the road. But the response belongs to the individual.
In this story the two arise from the meal table and return to Jerusalem. There is a sense of resurrection, of a new beginning about their action – they get up. They arise from their despair and they return to Jerusalem. They head out once more on the road but this time when they return to Jerusalem they are nourished by Christ's presence. They go back with the memory of their burning hearts – the passion at their centre that prompts and calls them to action. They now have the faith to understand the events that have happened. So they go back with a new energy and purpose – they go back, carrying their experience with them and

seeking out others with whom to share it. In that way they go back with a sense of mission and commission from the Risen Lord.

When we look to our Sunday experience, there is a real sense of resurrection for us also. In light of what we celebrate and profess in the Mass, we are called to get up – like these two on the road to Emmaus. We are called to arise out of our graves, out of our ways that are not life-giving or nourishing or sustaining. Through our active participation in the celebration of the Mass, our understanding of life and its meaning is shaped and changed. We carry the message of resurrection with us. Jesus died and rose again for us; in baptism we have the promise of this new life.

In light of this new life, we are continually being called and being sent. If we have heard the good news and have been fed by Christ in the Eucharist, then the impulse is to go and do this, go and be this, go and share this. The impulse is to move beyond the confines of the church building and reach out. In every Mass there is an exodus, a time of going out, and we go as people sent, sent to love and serve the Lord in the very ordinary stuff of our lives.

Silence – with reflection question
Facilitator: Imagine yourself at the end of a Sunday Mass. Where are you being sent to and what difference does what you just celebrated make?

Sharing
Facilitator: Invite participants to share with their neighbour one thought they had during the quiet time.

Sung response: Verse 5 of 'The Servant Song' by Richard Gillard
Facilitator/Prayer leader invites participants to stand *and join in singing one verse of this or another suitable hymn.*

'When we sing to God in heaven there will be such harmony;
Born of all we've known together of Christ's love and agony

Will you let me be your servant, let me be as Christ to you;
Pray that I may have the grace to let you be my servant too.'

Closing Opportunity for Sharing

The facilitator invites people to reflect on the following question for a couple of minutes with people around them.
» Is there some thought/action that you are taking with you from this time of reflection?
(After a couple of minutes, invite participants to come back to the large group, and ask if anybody would like to share a final comment/insight. Then invite people to tea at the end of the session and end with a closing prayer.)

Closing Prayer

Reflection on Eucharist

'There are so many hungry people in this world, and their hunger is more than physical. Children are starving for love and affection. The elderly are groaning out of loneliness. People in our families and circle of friends are craving our time and attention. The poor and sick yearn for care and understanding. The wealthy hunger for meaning. Our challenge as Eucharistic people is to become the Bread of Life for others.

'As St Augustine put it: "Become what you receive." We, as Christians, must become the bread that feeds the hungry people around us. We are called to feed others with love, care, compassion, concern, hospitality and justice. This is precisely what we commit ourselves to at each Eucharist. The challenge is addressed to each of us personally, and as a community: "The Body of Christ." "The Blood of Christ."

'When we say our "Amen", we accept the challenge. We say, "Yes! I am called to break my body and pour out my blood for everybody. Yes! I am daily bread for the hungry people I know and those I don't know." That "Amen" is one of the most important words we say at Mass. We should think twice before we say it. It should make us shudder.

'To receive the Eucharist is to make the commitment to become the Eucharist – for whoever needs it. Indeed, if we do not intend to "become what we receive", we would do well to absent ourselves from the communion line.'

(Oscar Romero)

and/or

'In each of our lives Jesus comes as the Bread of Life – to be eaten, to be consumed by us. This is how he loves us. Then Jesus comes in our human lives as the hungry one, the other, hoping to be fed with the Bread of our life, our hearts by loving, and our hands by serving. In loving and serving, we prove that we have been created in the likeness of our God, for God is love and when we love we are like God.

(Blessed Teresa of Calcutta)

Prayer

God of the night and God of the day
Be with us as we go from this place.
Give us a restful night
That we might wake renewed and refreshed
To arise and live our lives as Eucharist for one another.
We ask this through Christ our Lord. Amen.

EUCHARISTIC PRAYER II HANDOUT

V. The Lord be with you.
R. And with your spirit.
V. Lift up your hearts.
R. We lift them up to the Lord.
V. Let us give thanks to the Lord our God.
R. It is right and just.

It is truly right and just, our duty and our salvation,
always and everywhere to give you thanks, Father most holy,
through your beloved Son, Jesus Christ,
your Word through whom you made all things,
whom you sent as our Saviour and Redeemer,
incarnate by the Holy Spirit and born of the Virgin.
Fulfilling your will and gaining for you a holy people,
he stretched out his hands as he endured his Passion,
so as to break the bonds of death and manifest the resurrection.

And so, with the Angels and all the Saints
we declare your glory,
as with one voice we acclaim:

Holy, Holy, Holy Lord God of hosts.
Heaven and earth are full of your glory.
Hosanna in the highest.
Blessed is he who comes in the name of the Lord.
Hosanna in the highest.

You are indeed Holy, O Lord,
the fount of all holiness.
Make holy, therefore, these gifts, we pray,
by sending down your Spirit upon them like the dewfall,
so that they may become for us
the Body and ✠ Blood of our Lord Jesus Christ.

At the time he was betrayed
and entered willingly into his Passion,
he took bread and, giving thanks, broke it,
and gave it to his disciples, saying:
TAKE THIS, ALL OF YOU, AND EAT OF IT,
FOR THIS IS MY BODY,
WHICH WILL BE GIVEN UP FOR YOU.

In a similar way, when supper was ended,
he took the chalice
and, once more giving thanks,
he gave it to his disciples, saying:
TAKE THIS, ALL OF YOU, AND DRINK FROM IT,
FOR THIS IS THE CHALICE OF MY BLOOD,
THE BLOOD OF THE NEW AND ETERNAL COVENANT,
WHICH WILL BE POURED OUT FOR YOU AND FOR MANY
FOR THE FORGIVENESS OF SINS.
DO THIS IN MEMORY OF ME.

The mystery of faith.
We proclaim your Death, O Lord,
and profess your Resurrection
until you come again.
　Or:
When we eat this Bread and drink this Cup,
we proclaim your Death, O Lord,
until you come again.
　Or:
Save us, Saviour of the world,
for by your Cross and Resurrection
you have set us free.
　Or:
My Lord and my God.

Therefore, as we celebrate
the memorial of his Death and Resurrection,
we offer you, Lord,
the Bread of life and the Chalice of salvation,
giving thanks that you have held us worthy
to be in your presence and minister to you.

Humbly we pray
that, partaking of the Body and Blood of Christ,
we may be gathered into one by the Holy Spirit.

Remember, Lord, your Church,
spread throughout the world,
and bring her to the fullness of charity,
together with N. our Pope and N. our Bishop*
and all the clergy.

Remember also our brothers and sisters
who have fallen asleep in the hope of the resurrection,
and all who have died in your mercy:
welcome them into the light of your face.
Have mercy on us all, we pray,
that with the Blessed Virgin Mary, Mother of God,
with the blessed Apostles,
and all the Saints who have pleased you throughout the ages,
we may merit to be coheirs to eternal life,
and may praise and glorify you
through your Son, Jesus Christ.

Through him, and with him, and in him,
O God, almighty Father,
in the unity of the Holy Spirit,
all glory and honour is yours,
for ever and ever.
Amen.

This page may be photocopied

A Short Recommended Reading List

At the Supper of the Lamb: A Pastoral and Theological Commentary on the Mass, Paul Turner (Chicago: Liturgy Training Publications, 2011)

Celebrating the Mass – A Pastoral Introduction, Catholic Bishops' Conference of England and Wales (London: Catholic Truth Society, 2005)

Celebrating the Mass Throughout the Year – Eucharist and the Liturgical Year, National Centre for Liturgy (Dublin: Veritas, 2011)

Celebrating the Mystery of Faith – A Guide to the Mass (Revised Edition), National Centre for Liturgy (Dublin: Veritas, 2011)

General Instruction of the Roman Missal (Dublin: Veritas, 2005)

The Eucharist: Communion With Christ And With One Another; Theological and Pastoral Reflections in Preparation for the 50th International Eucharistic Congress, IEC 2012 (Dublin: Veritas, 2011)

The Roman Missal, Revised Third Edition (Dublin: Veritas, 2011)

Acknowledgements

This programme could not have been written without the active support of a large number of people who, in a variety of ways, helped bring it to fruition. I wish to take this opportunity to both acknowledge and to express my thanks to them.

While risking the exclusion of someone in error, I thank in particular the following:

Those brave and adventurous souls who took this material to the coalface in parishes across the diocese of Kildare & Leighlin and who in turn offered invaluable feedback, including: Fr Ger Ahern, Margarita Bedding, Mairead Darcy, Margaret Farrell, Ann Fleming, Gerard Gallagher, Shane Gallagher, Noeline Lynam, Elaine Mahon, Sr Mary Murphy RSM, Una Meehan, Geraldine Moore, Jean Moroney, Paddy O'Byrne, Fr Tom O'Byrne, Hazel O'Connor, Catherine Ryan, Sr Ann Walshe PBVM and Pamela Whelan.

My colleagues in Kildare & Leighlin Faith Development Services: Fr John Cummins, Sr Anne Holton RSM, Maeve Mahon, Robert Norton, Christine Oglesby and Yvonne Rooney for their ongoing companionship, witness and support, as well as to the staff of Bishop's House, Fr Bill Kemmy and Anna McLaren. Thank you also to Mgr Brendan Byrne (Diocesan Administer) for his leadership and continual encouragement. I would like to thank the retired Bishop Jim Moriarty who founded Kildare & Leighlin Faith Development Services and who over the years has been so affirming and supportive of our work.

Many thanks must go to the people of the diocese of Kildare & Leighlin, in particular those people involved in the Diocesan Interim Liturgy Commission, liturgy groups, baptism teams, parish pastoral councils and liturgical ministries, as well as to the faith leaders of the parishes of the diocese – priests and pastoral workers – and parish secretaries; it is both a sheer gift and privilege to have the opportunity to work with you.

Deep thanks and appreciation goes to Fr Paddy Jones and Fr Tom Whelan CSSp who took the time to read the final draft of this programme and to offer feedback and encouragement. Many thanks for the huge support and opportunities both have given to me over the years in ministry.

Thanks also to Fr Liam Tracey OSM and Sr Moira Bergin RSM who, together with Fr Paddy Jones, make up the staff of the National Centre for Liturgy. This Centre has had a tremendous role to play in my journey of working in the Church, since the day as a teenager I received an invitation to come to Mass at the Centre by the late and much missed Mgr Seán Swayne (founder of the Centre and priest of the diocese of Kildare & Leighlin) through my days as a student there under the direction of the late Fr Seán Collins OFM and beyond.

Many thanks also to Fr Gareth Byrne.

A final word of thanks to the staff at Veritas who have brought this book to publication, in particular to Caitriona Clarke, Colette Dower and Dara O'Connor for the work they have given to this project.